# FIRST STEPS IN VEGETARIAN COOKING

Lots of delicious and simple recipes, backed up with plenty of help
and advice, for every aspiring vegetarian.

*Front cover illustration:* Lentil and Tomato Bake (page 64).

# FIRST STEPS IN VEGETARIAN COOKING

*by*

KATHY SILK

*Illustrated by Ian Jones*

*Photography and styling by*
*Paul Turner and Sue Pressley*
*Stonecastle Graphics, Maidstone*
*Kent*

This edition published 1993 by
Diamond Books
77–85 Fulham Palace Road,
Hammersmith, London W6 8JB

First published 1979
Second edition, revised, expanded and reset, 1983

Printed in Great Britain by
HarperCollinsManufacturing Glasgow

# CONTENTS

|  |  | Page |
| --- | --- | --- |
| *Introduction* |  | 7 |
| *Chapter* |  |  |
| 1. | Your First ♈ Day | 11 |
| 2. | ♈ Day Guidelines | 15 |
| 3. | Basics | 23 |
| 4. | Soups and Starters | 34 |
| 5. | Snacks and Lunches | 39 |
| 6. | Your Evening Meal | 54 |
| 7. | Vegetables and Salads | 76 |
| 8. | Desserts | 85 |
|  | *Glossary* | 91 |
|  | *Useful Addresses* | 93 |
|  | *Where Can I Turn for Help?* | 94 |
|  | *Index* | 95 |

# INTRODUCTION

**Well, Why Don't Some People Eat Meat, Fish or Poultry?**
There are many reasons — ethical, aesthetic, religious, nutritional
and medical. Many people find that eating dead flesh is repugnant
to them. Many more question the morality of taking life for food.
They feel it is immoral to arrange purposely the conception of huge
numbers of animals, only to imprison them for most of their lives,
many in semi-darkness in overcrowded places. Many animals have
no room to move properly, are drugged, are fattened to provide more
meat, and are killed when unable to stand the strain of this and of
disease. Those that survive until they are the right size and weight
are herded into trucks for their last journey. No green fields and
pastures new for most of these.

Some people think that cows, sheep, pigs, birds and fish are there
specially for us to use in any way we choose, with no question of the
creatures having a choice. They don't even have a language we can
understand. But look into their eyes, see their fear when pushed
around, goaded into lorries, beaten with sticks to make them walk
along that final path to their own destruction, hear their bellowing,
bleating and squealing, and how can anyone say that it is fair, just,
moral or compassionate? Of course it isn't. Would they go to their
death from their own choice, do you think? Would you go the same
way, without a struggle?

Animals do not have the ability to communicate except by their
behavioural response to the way that we treat them. If there is fear
in their eyes, and they struggle and try to get away, isn't it wrong
to inflict great pain and to take away their lives? Animals know fear

and feel pain much as humans do — but sadly haven't the voice to protest loudly enough, for all to hear.

Some people say 'We are their masters, the animals are our slaves. We look after them well all their lives, and put them to death in as humane a way as possible'. What is humane about putting to death a creature who doesn't need to die, just so that it can be stripped of its skin for leather, its flesh for meat, its blood for fertilizer, its bones, horns and hooves for gelatine and glue?

How is it done? By using a captive bolt or free bullet humane-killer, and cutting its throat. A degrading and horrifying experience for anyone to gain their weekly wage by — who'd be a slaughterer? Well, if you won't be a slaughterer, why pay someone else to do the dirty work for you? You don't have to — you could stop eating meat.

Of course, some people have only just discovered the horrors of factory farming — and want no further part in it. So much has been written and filmed these past few years, that the number of people thinking about changing their diet is growing all the time, thankfully. The custom of meat-eating through habit and the tradition of the family you belong to, the instruction to 'eat up that lovely meat, it's good for you', has surely conditioned the lives of many.

How many parents hide from their children the knowledge that meat is the flesh of a calf, lamb or pig? Do they elaborate on the technique involved in arriving at the beefburger, lamb chop or sausage? I doubt it! How many adults know, or dare to think, about how the meat on their plates actually got there?

We don't need to eat the flesh of other creatures in order to stay alive or healthy. What would we do with all these excess creatures you may ask, if we stopped killing them for food? Well, in the first place, the same number of animals wouldn't be raised. At present, the farmer and his stockmen are supreme manipulative breeders. They plan to increase the numbers as much and as fast as they can to provide more meat and thus more profit. If we ate less meat as a nation, the farmer would have to reduce his breeding stations and factory farms. Would the price of meat rise to compensate for this? Yes, I believe it would. Which would mean that fewer people ate it, and would turn to other kinds of food.

Are we trying to relieve the farmer of his job? Not exactly. I am hoping that he will simply change the type of food he is growing. At the moment, he is growing animals — huge extra numbers of animals, who wouldn't be here if it weren't for breeding programmes. And first of all, we have to grow the grain (or import it) to feed animals which are then killed so that humans may eat the flesh. What a lot of work, waste and misery. Why not set out to grow the kinds of food that humans can eat, enjoy, and keep healthy on, without all the misery at present entailed.

If you have not yet read *Food for a Future* by Jon Wynne-Tyson, and *Animal Liberation* by Peter Singer, I recommend that you do — soon. These books will give much background information and are obtainable from bookshops, or from The Vegetarian Society, whose address is at the back of the book.

Many people feel that they only want to consume natural, wholesome, clean food, which improves and maintains their personal health, and want to see what a vegetarian diet can do for them.

Much has been written recently about diets of one kind or another. There has been a trend to eat less meat, less animal fat, less salt, less sugar; more fruit, more vegetables, more wholemeal flour products, and of course, more fibre! By removing all the meat, fish and poultry from a diet, and using more of the pulses or legumes, i.e. beans, lentils, peas, chick peas etc., and more nuts, cereals and wholegrain rice, we arrive at just what vegetarians have been eating all along, and for many generations. A vegetarian diet is naturally full of fibre, we don't need to increase it. We tend to use less salt and less sugar than most people, and we use vegetable oils and fats. It follows, then, that modern health trends are moving towards the vegetarian way of life. For most people, it is wise to allow the system to adjust slowly to changes, such as the increase in dietary fibre, or you may have a temporary digestive disturbance!

## Who Are These People? What Are They Like?
Just like you and me.

They are thinking, caring people who want to help lessen the unnecessary cruelty and exploitation of animals — with the added bonus of improving their own health. People from all walks of life have changed to a vegetarian style of eating and are enjoying it. You could too. Another bonus is that your expenditure on food could be much less on a vegetarian diet.

Vegetarianism is not new. The ancient Greeks lived on it. From Pythagoras, Socrates, Leonardo da Vinci, Tolstoy, General and Mrs Bramwell Booth, to those in living memory, such as George Bernard Shaw and Mahatma Gandhi, many of the best minds have been advocates of vegetarianism. Today, in the public eye, we have Brigid Brophy, Kate Bush, Julie Christie, Barbara Dickson, Lady Dowding, Judy Geeson, Beryl Grey, George Harrison, Dr Kenneth Kaunda, Cheryl Kennedy, Carla Lane, Malcolm Muggeridge, Paul and Linda McCartney, Virginia McKenna, John Peel, Richard Ryder, William Shatner, Martin Shaw, Malcolm Stoddard, Dennis Weaver and The Rt. Hon. Bernard Weatherill, M.P., Speaker of the House of Commons, amongst many others.

It must also be said that perhaps half the population of the world may be living on a vegetarian diet through necessity.

The word 'vegetarian' is derived from the Latin *vegetus* which means, whole, fresh, full of life.

**What Do They Eat Instead?**
An abundance of delicious foods. Fruits, vegetables, nuts — hazels, peanuts, walnuts, almonds; seeds such as sunflower, sesame, and pumpkin; pulses (legumes), which include haricot (navy) beans, soya, black-eye, pinto, flageolet, red kidney and butter beans, chick peas (garbanzos), split peas, lentils etc.; wholegrain rice, wholewheat spaghetti, macaroni and lasagne etc. Textured vegetable protein, cheese and other milk products, free-range eggs and plant milk (made from soya beans) and tofu (soya beancurd) are also used by some to add to the above range of foods, as well as all herbs and spices.

Why eat these particular things? Because we like them and we believe that these foods are healthy to eat. And because we cannot condone the cruelty involved in the production of flesh foods.

The change to a vegetarian diet is a first step to help yourself and the voiceless creatures. They have no-one to speak for them but us. So how about it? Will you start to help by having a Y Day once a week?

# 1.
# YOUR FIRST ♈ DAY

## How Should I Go About It?
Start by having a ♈ Day once a week. ♈ for Vegetarian Day, that is!

Then go on to two ♈ Days a week, then three ♈ Days a week a little later on, increasing at your own rate.

## When Shall I Try?
Why not get ready for your first ♈ Day tomorrow? (Of course, if you are a very busy person, then start collecting items as soon as you can!)

## Here is Your ♈ Day Plan:
Begin the day with a small glass of unsweetened orange or grapefruit juice. Make a fruity muesli from rolled oats, a spoonful of soaked sultanas or raisins, grated apple, grated nuts, and milk or fruit juice to moisten. There are also ready-made varieties of muesli, which simply need fresh fruit and liquid added, but do try and choose one without sugar, if you can. For more variations of muesli, see page 29. Then have a slice of wholemeal bread or a roll, spread with polyunsaturated margarine for preference, or with butter. You could add peanut butter, hazelnut butter, a thin spread of vegetable yeast extract (*Barmene, Tastex* or *Marmite*), or marmalade made with dark sugar, or one of the new sugarless jams.

If you prefer a cooked breakfast, have mushrooms, tomatoes or baked beans on wholemeal toast, but do have some fruit or fruit juice first.

For lunch at home, how about Cheese and Apple Toast (page 46), or curried beans on toast with watercress and sliced tomatoes. For a packed lunch, try a bean, tomato and chive paste sandwich, and pack lettuce hearts and celery sticks to eat with it. Add an apple, pear or orange, and fruit juice to drink.

For your evening meal, how about:

Grapefruit juice, tomato juice or Julienne Soup (page 37)
Pan Haggerty (page 50) with watercress, celery and beetroot salad
Pears in Cinnamon Sauce (page 88)

or:

Pineapple, carrot and cress salad
Chinese Stir-Fry with almonds and rice (page 51)
Apricot and Apple Delight (page 88)

There are more ideas for lunches at home on page 44, packed lunches on page 53, and evening meals on page 54.

What will you need in your store cupboard to start with?

*Breakfast:* Either fresh, tinned or bottled fruit juice, or fruit. Ready-packed muesli with nuts and fruit, or keep a packet of mixed muesli base cereals, and add your own dried fruit and nuts as needed. Or simply use rolled oats as a base. A small bag of mixed shelled nuts, or 2 or 3 bags of shelled nuts of the type you like. A small bag of raw cane sugar (if you must), either Barbados, Muscovado or Demerara, but please use it very sparingly!

Small bags of dried fruit — raisins, sultanas, dates, figs, apricots, prunes, bananas etc.

For mixing the muesli or cereal, use milk, plantmilk (soya bean milk) tinned or in cartons, or fruit juice.

Wheatgerm if liked; bran if required; wholemeal rolls, bread or wholewheat crispbread. Polyunsaturated margarine or butter.

Vegetable yeast extract, such as *Barmene, Tastex* or *Marmite.* Real peanut butter or hazelnut butter (without added salt or sugar), marmalade and sugarless jam, if used.

Most of these items will last for many ⋎ Day breakfasts.

*Lunch and Evening Meal:* Choose ideas and recipes from each section, and check to see if you have the appropriate items in store. If not, list them after your breakfast ones, and head for the shops!

A big yet very easy step.

## ᛉ Day Menus

Here are some menus for you to consider for your first ᛉ Day evening meal.

Minty Green Pea Soup (page 36)
Golden Slice (page 56), creamed potatoes, runner beans and sliced
 tomatoes
Pears in Cinnamon Sauce (page 88)

Avocado with tomato slices and dressing
Sesame and Brazil Nut Roast (page 54) with Bircher Potatoes (page
 70), garden peas and rich brown sauce (page 32)
Fresh fruit salad (page 85)

Tomato Juice
Celery hearts au gratin (crumbs, nuts, seeds/cheese mixture on top
 of dish, put under grill) jacket potatoes (page 77), carrots and
 watercress
Compote of dried fruits — pears, apricots, figs etc., soaked overnight
 in fruit juice

Pineapple juice
Fruity Black-eye Beans (page 57), rice and green salad
Small bunch of fresh grapes

Grapefruit juice
Mushroom Pizza (page 66), jacket potatoes (page 77), Celery Coleslaw
 (page 78)
Fresh fruit — peaches, plums or soft fruit

Hummus (page 41) with wholewheat crispbreads or tomato juice
Cheese and Rice Croquettes (page 59), Cauliflower, Carrot and
 Cucumber Salad (page 80), with tomatoes and watercress
Apricot and Apple Delight (page 88)

Corn on the cob (page 76 ) or Avocado and Orange Salad (page 78)
Stuffed Mushrooms (page 67), broccoli, garden peas with chives,
 Bircher Potatoes (page 77)
Baked Bananas with Plum Sauce (page 87)

Guacomole Dip (page 42) or fruit juice
Almond and Potato Loaf, (page 62) Beetroot and Apple Salad (page 79), cucumber and watercress
Fruit jelly (page 86) and Cashewnut Cream (page 89)

Leek and Carrot Soup (page 34) or grapefruit juice
Nutty Fries (page 49) with chutney, creamed potatoes and spring greens or green salad and tomatoes
Fresh peaches or apricots with raspberries, or yogurt

Winter Salad (page 80)
Macaroni Cheese Special (page 60) and runner beans
Apple and Date Whip (page 86)

Tomato Soup (page 35)
Aduki-burgers (page 58), Chinese Salad (page 82), sliced beetroot and watercress (page 44) Peach flan

Half a fresh grapefruit
Lentil and Tomato Bake (page 64), caraway cabbage (page 76), jacket potatoes (page 77)
Apple Pie and Cashewnut Cream (page 89)

Apple juice
Ratatouille (page 63), wholemeal bread and cheese, green salad
Fresh sliced oranges and bananas in orange juice

Honeydew melon with redcurrants or ginger
Chick peas with rice (page 71), green salad
Apple *purée* with raisins and flaked almonds

Apple juice
Cashew and Mushroom Curry (page 72), mango chutney and green salad
Fresh pineapple slices

# 2.

# ⋎ DAY GUIDELINES

When choosing food to buy for yourself or your family, it's as well to bear the following in mind.

The more raw food you eat, the more vitamins, minerals and roughage you will obtain for your better health — in other words, a large raw salad with a protein savoury is best for everyone, whenever possible.

When you cook vegetables, use only a little water, cut the vegetables small, add little or no salt, and short-cook them, or steam or bake them. You may be surprised at the good, natural flavour that has previously been masked by salt and lost by overcooking. Either drink the cooking liquid, or keep it covered in a refrigerator for up to 24 hours, and boil again before using it as stock in sauces, soups and casseroles. The minerals from the vegetables are in the water — don't waste them by throwing it away. Don't always peel root vegetables, just scrub them well under running water before cooking. With all fresh fruit, vegetables and salad material, it is most important to wash all items very thoroughly to help remove any chemical residues. If you can grow some of your own vegetables, salads, fruit and herbs on naturally composted soil, so much the better.

Use wholemeal bread and flour — it's tastier and more satifying. Although there are mineral traces in all 'dark' sugars — and none at all in white — use it very sparingly anyway. Try eating whole fruit rather than always only extracting the juice and discarding the healthy fibre. Obviously citrus fruit and bananas are exceptions, do peel those first! Chewing is also good for the teeth, gums and jaws, and aids digestion as well as bringing about the feeling of satiety or fullness.

It is also important that food should look appealing, and be pleasantly aromatic. An apple a day or more, still makes sense, and add to that an orange a day as well.

When buying prepared, packaged and tinned food, get into the habit of reading labels. Many sweet and savoury biscuits and crackers, cakes, breads and pastry, contain animal fat or marine oil. They need to be checked each time you buy, as manufacturers are continually changing their recipes. If there is a long list of chemical additives on the label, think twice about buying it. (See the Shopper's Guide section of the Vegetarian Society's handbook.)

Avoid using products which contain monosodium glutamate. This is the white, powdered crystals of glutamic acid. Tasteless in itself, this product enhances the flavours of other foods, but it is known to cause allergic reactions in many people, so should be avoided if possible.

Avoid products labelled 'edible fat', 'shortening' or just 'margarine', as these are not clearly defined as being non-animal fat.

Next time you shop buy 100% vegetable oil, white vegetable fat (there are several brands) and polyunsaturated margarines (without whale oil), instead of lard, suet, and mixed oil margarines, and free-range eggs instead of battery-raised eggs, if you use them. The family won't notice anything but a lovely difference in taste.

Do your best not to increase the amount of dairy produce you eat i.e. cheese, butter and cream, as they have a high content of saturated fat, which could be unwise for your health if consumed in large amounts. Instead, gradually replace the meat, poultry and fish in your diet with nut and cereal dishes, or beans, lentils, chick peas (garbanzos) and rice etc. or textured vegetable protein. This latter product is made from soya beans, is high in protein, and is easy and economical to make up. Just follow the directions on the packet. Soya 'mince', 'chunks', 'burgers', and 'sausages' etc. can be used in place of meat in many conventional recipes such as shepherd's pie, burgers, and bolognese sauce etc.

If you include the recipes and ideas suggested here, it is unlikely that you will be short of protein, iron and other minerals, or Vitamin $B_{12}$ (contained in dairy products, yeast extract with $B_{12}$, plantmilks with $B_{12}$, some kinds of textured vegetable protein etc.) which are often queried in connection with the vegetarian diet. A vegan diet (where no animal products at all are consumed i.e. no meat, fish, poultry, eggs or any dairy products) is the diet where Vitamin $B_{12}$ may be short, and vegans know this, and eat products which have added Vitamin $B_{12}$, or take a supplement.

With more and more people changing their diet from white to wholemeal bread, and using polyunsaturated margarine instead of butter and cheaper hard margarines, it is becoming much easier for the newcomer to vegetarian fare to tell relatives and friends that they have made even further changes to their diet. People talk a great deal about food these days — the price of it, the quality and availability, and all the new cookery books concerned with the new style of eating, such as less meat, less animal fat, sugar and salt, and the use of wholegrain products. Television and radio programmes, newspaper and magazine articles abound with news and views, recipes and suggestions. So you should be able to bring up the subject much more easily than those who became vegetarians many years ago.

If you are a young person who has someone else to cook for you at home, it will be wise to 'go easy' at first about the changes in shopping and preparation involved. If you are keen to become a vegetarian, you must show willing to devise menus, and assist with the shopping and the cooking, otherwise the cook in your household may not be as enthusiastic as yourself. Do not be critical of past food consumed at home. After all, most of us had to find out at some stage about how our food found its way to the table.

Your introduction of the idea of vegetarian food into the house should be a quiet revelation, not an overpowering revolution. You may still be the only one who wants to eat this way, now and for some time to come. So be gentle, firm and encouraging to others.

When you are invited out to a meal, say at a friend's home, it is only courtesy to tell them well in advance that your diet is different now, and it may be easier for you to write a note to this effect, giving one or two suggestions perhaps, or else saying that you will chat to them on the telephone about it, if you're shy. If you have a vegetarian restaurant near you, visit it when you can, and take your friends there to show them what kind of meals you are now eating. When invited to a formal dinner at a conventional hotel or restaurant, it is wise to write about two weeks in advance, and also to telephone them two days beforehand as a reminder. State clearly what you cannot eat, then leave it to the caterer to use their imagination, or to ask you specifically what you would like. Some caterers do not like their menu planned for them!

Most schools allow packed lunches to be brought in these days. If you are at college or university, you may wish to rally other like-minded students (I'm sure there'll be some) to approach the catering manager with some interesting ideas — and great tact. There are now several vegetarian catering only halls in UK universities.

Cooking for yourself in a flat or bedsitter does mean planning ahead, and perhaps having to include more ready-prepared bought food, as well as more raw food, if cooking facilities are inadequate.

If you are the cook of the house, and are interested in changing your diet, you really need to go easy on the others for whom you prepare meals, and not necessarily go into details about your $\vee$ Days, if you think it might cause alarm. Let your family think you have become more adventurous, but don't try too many 'different' foods all at once.

The Vegetarian Society publishes a Catering Leaflet which should be of great help to hand to anyone who is going to prepare food for you, such as the college caterer, guest house, hotel or restaurant (if you haven't chosen a vegetarian one!), airline, cruise ship, or hospital, as well as friends and relatives. Write for details, with a stamped addressed envelope, to the address at the back of the book.

It is recognized by the Department of Health and Social Security that a vegetarian diet should be provided, on request in advance, in all State Hospitals.

Do feel that you can complain if meals out of the home are inadequate, or simply awful. On the other hand, do remember to say thank you, with a big smile, when you are pleased with what you are served, as we want to encourage caterers. Remember, someone else is a customer the next day — it might be me! When travelling, it is just as well to have a snack meal and/or fruit and nuts etc., with you.

The Vegetarian Society runs several kinds of cookery courses at their headquarters in Altrincham near Manchester (see page 94) — weekly residential plus evening and weekend courses for all kinds of wholefood vegetarian cookery, i.e. for home, hotel, school catering or to learn demonstration. Send two first class stamps and a stamped addressed envelope for a list of their courses and others around the country. Ask at your local library or town hall for possible classes near to you.

The Vegetarian Society membership is divided into branches across the country. If there is a branch near you, why not become a Member, or Associate Member (if you are not a full-time vegetarian, but are sympathetic to the aims of the Society)? That way, you can get to know like-minded people with whom to discuss ideas, recipes etc. They will also be able to give help and support if you are a newcomer to vegetarianism.

Here are just a few of the less obvious, but no less important, ideas and guidelines which you should bear in mind. When you meet other, long-standing vegetarians, they will no doubt share many more with you.

*We like to use* 100% vegetable oils, e.g. corn oil, sunflower oil, sesame, olive, soya, groundnut oil etc., for cooking and making salad dressings.

*We like to use* 100% polyunsaturated vegetable margarines or butter for spreading and cooking. 100% white vegetable fats such as *Trex, Pura, White Flora, Suenut* and *Nutter* for cooking are widely available. We do not use lard, suet, dripping or animal-based white cooking fats.

*We like to use* agar-agar (a fine white odourless, tasteless powder) or carragheen moss (flakes or pieces), which are made from seaweeds, when making savoury or sweet jellies. Prepared fruit jellies needing only fruit juice or water to be added, can be obtained at health food stores. We do not use gelatine or usual jelly blocks or crystals, which are made from animal bones and hides.

*We like to use* free-range eggs instead of battery farm raised eggs, if they are used at all. These are becoming more widely available, but don't be misled by advertising slogans, such as 'farm fresh' or 'country fresh', etc., which are not the same thing.

*We like to use* vegetable stock cubes (concentrated flavour with minerals from vegetables), which can be bought at health food stores, and we don't use the so-called 'meaty' ones available elsewhere. Home-made stock is easily made by using well-washed and trimmed outside leaves, stalks of tough vegetables, peelings etc., boiling these for about 45 minutes, straining the vegetables, and using the liquid for soups, casseroles and savoury sauces. Or use vegetable cooking water as indicated elsewhere.

*Many of us like to use* rennet-free cheese, which is cheese made with a vegetable enzyme instead of the usual rennet (from a calf's stomach). Rennet-free cheese is obtainable from health food stores, as well as the vegetable enzyme for home cheese-making.

If you have as great a variety as you can of these natural, wholesome foods, as suggested in this book, obtaining the best quality you can afford, preparing the fresh ones just before use, short-cooking where possible and making your meals look attractive as well as taste delicious, you will benefit enormously from the change to ℣ Day eating.

*Note:* At the time of going to press, the branded products referred to in this book were completely vegetarian in content. However, no guarantees can be given that they remain so and reference to the Shopper's Guide section of the International Vegetarian Handbook, and also the labels on the products, is advised.

## Storage of Food

*Flour:* Wholemeal, 81% and 85% (bran partially removed), should be bought in small amounts, stored in a cool, dark place and used up quickly, as it goes rancid more quickly than refined white flour. It may have been stored some time before you buy it, so use it within 6 weeks at most.

*Yeast:* Dried yeast in a vacuum-sealed tin will keep several months unopened. Once opened use up within 6 weeks. If it doesn't become frothy after mixing with water and waiting 15 minutes, it will not raise bread dough. Fresh yeast, if moist and smooth, will keep for up to 2 weeks in a screw-top jar in the refrigerator. Do not use if badly discoloured and dry.

*Grains, Pulses and Cereals:* Nuts, beans, muesli, lentils etc., all need to be bought in fairly small packs, dated and used up quickly. Store in a cool, dark but airy place in covered containers.

*Herbs and Spices:* Store in glass jars, covered with paper, labelled clearly with uses, dated, and stored away from sunlight in cool dark place. Buy small amounts, use up and replace.

*Vegetables and Fruit:* Only buy small amounts. Store in cool, dry airy place, away from a steamy kitchen. Leaf vegetables such as cabbage, cauliflower, and lettuce keep well in the salad drawer of the refrigerator.

Do try and get into the habit of dating your canned and packaged food, and new contents of storage jars etc., as you put them away, and turn out your food storage cupboards every few weeks to check the dates.

## Basic Tools in a Vegetarian Kitchen

Two chopping boards — one for bread, fruit etc., one for onions, leeks etc. (or use one board clearly marked bread or savoury side); Large and small sharp knives; mouli-mill (rotary-grater), or coffee grinder (kept for nuts etc.); four-sided upright grater; vegetable scrubbing brush; scissors; wire sieve; wooden and metal spoons; potato masher; lemon/orange squeezer; wire whisk; baking trays; ovenproof dishes; loaftins; bowls or basins of various sizes and a tin opener. A set of saucepans and frying pan (stainless steel, enamelled, or cast iron, if you are about to buy some). Avoid aluminium which can have a toxic effect. If you can manage any of the list below as well, you'll be all set fair.

Kitchen timer; rolling pin; wire rack; steamer; soup ladle; grapefruit knife; pestle and mortar; and a liquidizer or food processor.

## Where to Buy and What to Buy

The following items may be bought in health food shops and many of them also in wholefood shops, and will give you a wide range of foods to choose from and experiment with, together with all the recipes and ideas in this book.

Vegetable pâtés in tins, tubes and jars, plain or with herbs. Soya bean pâté; mushroom pâté in jars. Sugarless jams; marmalade with dark sugar; honey of all kinds; peanut butter, smooth or crunchy (without added salt and sugar); vegetable concentrates for spreading and making hot drinks (similar to yeast extract).

Cereals — wheat; rye; barley; oats; oatmeal (fine, pinhead or medium, and coarse) for baking, savouries and muesli; bran; wheatgerm; ready mixed muesli (some without sugar); wholewheat flakes; wholewheat pasta.

Carob powder; vegetable enzyme liquid for junket and cheese-making; vegetarian table jelly crystals; desserts.

Soup mixes; stock cubes; gravy mixes; sea vegetables.

In tins and foil packets — savoury vegetable protein in various sauces (chilli mix, curry mix, burger mix etc.); vegetarian ravioli.

Salad dressings; soya sauce; miso; vegetable oils.

Seeds; nuts; dried fruit; snack bars; crispbreads; biscuits; soyamilk; tofu; yeast.

Many of the above shops also sell wholemeal bread and rolls, and free-range eggs, and suet-free Christmas Pudding and minced fruit.

In your local supermarket or grocer, you may find the following very useful store cupboard items:

Tinned tomatoes; chick peas (garbanzo beans); red kidney beans; cannellini beans; celery hearts; artichokes; sweet corn; asparagus; mushrooms; ratatouille; red peppers; pease pudding; stuffed aubergines (eggplants); tomato *purée* and lentils in tomato juice. There is more tinned fruit in its own juice or apple juice now available.

Do read all labels carefully, and consider whether you need foods with added salt, sugar and preservatives. Whatever you decide to eat — I do hope that you will enjoy it!

# 3.

# BASICS

## BEANS
### Preparation Chart

| TYPE OF BEAN | SOAKING TIME (HOURS) | COOKING TIME HOURS) |
|---|---|---|
| Soya beans | 20-24 | 2-2½ |
| Chick peas (garbanzos) | ,, | 2 |
| Dried whole green peas | ,, | 1½-2 |
| Black beans | ,, | 1½-2 |
| Pinto beans | ,, | 1½ |
| Red kidney beans* | ,, | 1-1½ |
| Haricot (navy) beans | ,, | 1-1¼ |
| Butter (Lima) beans | ,, | 1-1¼ |
| Flageolet beans | ,, | 1 |
| Aduki (Adzuki) beans (small red, Japanese) | 3 | 1-1¼ |
| Mung (Moong) beans (small green, Chinese) | ,, | 1-1¼ |
| Brown/green whole lentils (Continental) | ,, | 1-1¼ |
| Yellow or green split peas | ,, | 1-1¼ |
| Black-eye beans | — | ½ |
| Red split lentils | — | ¼-½ |

*Red Kidney beans must be boiled vigorously for 10 minutes, before turning down to simmer for another 1 hour 20 minutes until tender. Failure to do this may result in severe stomach upset due to toxins in the beans.

Never eat raw dried beans or undercooked beans. Some cooks suggest that bean soaking water should be drained and fresh water used to cook them, to help avoid flatulence. Check water level occasionally, add boiling water, if needed. Always add salt approximately 10 minutes before end of cooking time, otherwise the bean skins toughen and take longer to cook.

Ready-cooked tinned beans such as red kidney, cannellini, chick peas (garbanzos), haricot (navy) and butter (Lima) beans, need to be drained and rinsed before use, as the water is usually very salty. These tinned beans, lentils in tomato juice and pease pudding, are available at most grocers and supermarkets, and are useful if you are short of time.

## BROWN RICE

Long grain rice is usually chosen for savoury dishes and salads, and short grain for sweet dishes and sometimes risotto.

## PLAIN BOILED BROWN RICE

1.  Wash the rice well in a sieve under running water.

2.  Put twice its volume of water into a large saucepan, i.e. 2 cupsful of water for every cupful of rice.

3.  Bring water to the boil add rice and pinch of salt, put on lid, turn down to very low simmer, and leave for 35-40 minutes. Do not stir. If you suspect that the water has boiled away too fast, test a few grains by biting in half when cool. If not cooked, add a little more boiling water, replace lid and allow to cook a little longer.

# FRIED AND BOILED BROWN RICE

1. After washing rice, drain well, and add to one tablespoonful of vegetable oil heating in a large saucepan.

2. Fry gently, stirring carefully for 2 minutes. Add salt, and twice the volume (of rice) of boiling water or vegetable stock.

3. Stir once, put on lid when boiling, turn down to very low simmer for 35-40 minutes. Test and proceed as previous recipe when cooking time is up.

*Note:* If rice doesn't cook to tender in this time it may be 'old' rice. With next batch, after washing as above, put the rice in a large basin, fill with boiling water, cover with a large plate, and leave for 1 hour. Drain well and continue as per recipe.

Leftover cooked rice is very useful to add to soups, savouries, fritters and salad mixtures. Fresh or dried herbs, turmeric or saffron are often added during cooking for flavour and colour.

## SEEDS FOR SPROUTING

Many seeds and grains can be sprouted for use fresh or lightly cooked, in soups, sandwiches, pancakes, burgers, and Chinese stir-fry meals, or as a garnish on cooked dishes and salads.

Buy seeds only from a healthfood or wholefood store, not from a seed merchant unless labelled for sprouting to eat.

Try one of these four easy ones first:

| | |
|---|---|
| Aduki (Adzuki) beans (small red, Japanese) | — Use when 1½-2 in. (3-5cm) long |
| Mung (Moong) beans (small green, Chinese) | — As above |
| Alfalfa (Lucerne Grass) (very fine seed) | — As above |
| Wheat grains | — Use when ½-¾ in. (1-1.5cm) long |

1. Put one level tablespoonful of one of the beans, or of the wheat, into clean glass jars. (With alfalfa, use one teaspoonful only.)

2. Fill each jar with tepid water and leave overnight.

3. Cut a piece of muslin or fine net to amply cover the top of the jar plus 2 in. (5cm), secure with an elastic band, and drain the water away from the seeds through this.

4. Three or four times each day, fill the jar with tepid water and empty again straight away. Do not leave excess water in the jar or the beans or seeds will go musty, but they do need regular rinsing.

5. When they have grown to the length suggested above, tip them into a sieve and gently wash once more and serve. If they are not needed right away, put them in a bowl, covered, in the refrigerator. They will keep without growing any more for a few days. They can be used raw as they are, or lightly cooked in a little water or oil and soya sauce, but only for one minute or so!

## TO ROAST NUTS AND SEEDS

Spread shelled whole nuts on a shallow baking tray, and put in medium oven for about 10-15 minutes, stirring occasionally. Sunflower seeds and pumpkin seeds are also roasted as above, but sesame seeds need only 8 minutes or less. These seeds are bought at a health food or wholefood store, not a seed merchant.

Allow nuts or seeds to cool, and keep in an airtight container in cool place, and use up quickly. Use roasted nuts and seeds in place of raw ones, to give a change of flavour to nut spreads and nut roasts. Chopped or grated, they can be sprinkled over salads etc.

## TO BLANCH WHOLE ALMONDS

The skins of almonds are rather tough, and a recipe often calls for blanched almonds; it's very easy to do, thankfully, so here's how.

Put almonds in a small basin, pour on boiling water, leave for 5 minutes, drain, add cold water to cover, drain again, and pinch each almond between thumb and forefinger, and the skin will slip off easily.

## TO REMOVE SKINS FROM TOMATOES

Pour boiling water over fruit in a large basin, to completely cover them. Leave for 2 minutes (4-5 minutes for thicker-skinned fruits such as peaches, apricots and plums). Tip away water, pour in cold water, leave for 30 seconds, pierce each fruit with the point of a sharp knife and peel away skin with fingers. Tomatoes may also be skinned by piercing one at a time with a fork, and holding it over a gas flame with great care, turning the fork slowly till the skin 'pops'. Cool, then remove skin as above.

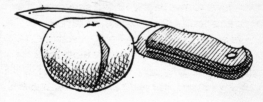

# WHOLEMEAL PASTRY

| Imperial (Metric) | American |
|---|---|
| 6 oz (170g) plain wholemeal flour | 1½ cupsful plain wholewheat flour |
| ½ level teaspoonful sea salt | ½ level teaspoonful sea salt |
| 3 oz (85g) white vegetable fat | ⅓ cupful white vegetable fat |
| About 2 tablespoonsful cold water | About 2 tablespoonsful cold water |

1.  Mix flour and salt and rub in fat to make 'breadcrumbs'.

2.  Add water gradually, and gather together into one firm piece. Leave in basin, cover and put in refrigerator for 30 minutes, if possible.

3.  Roll out pastry onto a floured surface, to the size and shape required, using a little flour from dredger if it is sticking to rolling pin or surface.

*Note:* The resulting pastry is sufficient to cover an 8 in. (20cm) flan case, or 4 small patty tins.

If you are new to wholemeal flour and find it difficult to use, then sieve out the bran, which will make an easier pastry to roll out. (Use the sieved bran on cereal or in savouries.) Or you can buy 81% or 85% flour, which has had some of the bran removed already.

# MUESLI

Muesli isn't just for breakfast, it can be a good meal in a bowl whenever you are in a rush and haven't time to cook! It is a nourishing meal for young or old alike.

*Ingredients for one person:*

**Imperial (Metric)**
1 tablespoonful rolled oats or mixed muesli base
1 tablespoonful grated nuts
1 tablespoonful raisins or chopped dates (soaked in juice)
1 medium dessert apple, grated
A little dark raw cane sugar (optional)
Milk or soyabean milk (or water or fruit juice or yogurt) to mix

**American**
1 tablespoonful rolled oats or mixed muesli base
1 tablespoonful grated nuts
1 tablespoonful raisins or chopped dates (soaked in juice)
1 medium dessert apple, grated
A little dark raw cane sugar (optional)
Milk or soybean milk (or water or fruit juice or yogurt) to mix

1.  Mix all ingredients in a basin using just enough chosen liquid to make a soft mixture.

*Note:* A squeeze of lemon juice may be added, and any other soaked, chopped dried fruit, as well as fresh chopped or grated fruit in season, to make variety all the year round. For instance, in the summer soft fruit season, make a strawberry, peach, raspberry, redcurrant or blackberry muesli — it's delicious. In the winter use apple *purée*, chopped pears, stewed prunes or soaked dried apricots or figs, or soaked and chopped dried bananas. A spoonful of wheatgerm or bran can be stirred in as well if required. Some people prefer to soak the oats, or other cereal, overnight (without additions) and add other ingredients and more liquid just before serving. Wash dried fruit well, and soak in water or fruit juice overnight. Some fruit may need a little cooking (prunes, figs) to tenderize, but avoid adding sugar. Raw or roasted seeds (sesame, sunflower or pumpkin) may be used instead of nuts.

# BASIC WHITE SAUCE

| Imperial (Metric) | American |
|---|---|
| 1 oz (30g) polyunsaturated margarine | 2½ tablespoonsful polyunsaturated margarine |
| 1 oz (30g) plain wholemeal flour | ¼ cupful plain wholewheat flour |
| ½ pint (285ml) milk or soyamilk | 1⅓ cupsful milk or soymilk |
| Pinch of sea salt and black pepper | Pinch of sea salt and black pepper |

1.  Melt margarine gently and stir in flour.

2.  Keep stirring over gentle heat to cook the flour for 3-4 minutes.

3.  Remove from heat, and gradually add the milk stirring all the time.

4.  Put back on the heat, and bring to boil still stirring, till thickened. Add salt and pepper.

*Note:* Use this sauce over vegetables such as fennel, courgettes (zucchini), carrots, broad (Windsor) beans etc. as a side dish when no other sauce is served at the meal. A teaspoonful or more of made mustard added with the milk makes a tastier sauce. Chopped parsley, chervil or summer savory or other herbs of choice can be included too. If grated cheese is added to the sauce, and poured over a cooked cauliflower, broccoli or celery hearts, or a mixture of cooked vegetables, topped with breadcrumbs, and a few nuts or seeds, you have yet another main course!

# WHISKED WHITE SAUCE

1.  Ingredients are as Basic White Sauce, but put them all into the saucepan at once.

2.  Put on gentle heat, and whisk with a wire whisk all the time. Gradually increase the heat, and boil for 2 minutes, still whisking.

3.  Remove from heat, add herbs or cheese or made mustard as before.

*Note:* If you stop whisking, it will go lumpy. If it goes lumpy, pour through a sieve, and put in clean pan and don't stop whisking this time!

# RICH QUICK CHEESE SAUCE

| Imperial (Metric) | American |
|---|---|
| 1 small tin evaporated milk | 1 small can evaporated milk |
| 2 tablespoonsful grated cheese | 2 tablespoonsful grated cheese |
| 1 heaped teaspoonful made mustard | 1 heaped teaspoonful made mustard |

1.  Open tin of milk, empty into small pan rinsed with water.

2.  Add the grated cheese and mustard, stir over gentle heat till melted.


# TOMATO SAUCE

| Imperial (Metric) | American |
|---|---|
| 1 oz (30g) polyunsaturated margarine | 2½ tablespoonsful polyunsaturated margarine |
| 1 small onion | 1 small onion |
| 6 large tomatoes | 6 large tomatoes |
| ½ pint (285ml) water | 1⅓ cupsful water |
| Pinch of sea salt, black pepper and raw cane sugar | Pinch of sea salt, black pepper and raw cane sugar |
| 2 bay leaves | 2 bay leaves |
| 1 tablespoonful finely chopped parsley | 1 tablespoonful finely chopped parsley |

1.  Chop onion and tomatoes and fry gently in heated margarine.

2.  Add water, salt, pepper, sugar, bay leaves and simmer for 15 minutes. Remove bay leaves and discard.

3.  Mash the sauce with a potato masher, or liquidize in a blender, or push through a wire sieve over a basin, with a spoon. Add parsley, reheat and serve.

*Note:* Delicious with many savouries or on vegetables.

## TANGY SAUCE

Make Tomato Sauce as above, adding the juice of an orange and 3 teaspoonsful soya sauce.

## RICH BROWN SAUCE

| Imperial (Metric) | American |
|---|---|
| 2 tablespoonsful vegetable oil | 2 tablespoonsful vegetable oil |
| 1 tablespoonful wholemeal flour | 1 tablespoonful wholewheat flour |
| 1 dessertspoonful soya flour | 2 teaspoonsful soy flour |
| ½ pint (285ml) hot vegetable stock or water | 1⅓ cupsful hot vegetable stock or water |
| 1 rounded teaspoonful vegetable yeast extract | 1 rounded teaspoonful vegetable yeast extract |

1.  Warm oil in a large saucepan. Add the flours and mix well.

2.  Add the hot liquid slowly, stirring all the time.

3.  Add yeast extract (*Barmene, Tastex* or *Marmite*) and stir well.

4.  Bring to the boil and simmer for 3 minutes.

*Note:* Serve as a sauce or gravy with nut savouries.

*In order of sequence:*
1.  Lentil Paste (page 40), Hummus (page 41), and Guacamole Dip (page 42).
2.  Bean, Tomato and Rice Salad (page 79), Chinese Salad (page 82) and Winter Salad (page 80).
3.  Fresh and Tangy Starters (page 38).
4.  Stuffed Vegetables (pages 67-9).

# BREADCRUMBS, CRUMBLES AND CROUTONS

When wholemeal bread isn't available, try *Vitawheat* and *Ryvita* crisp-breads. Any of these crispbreads, as well as whole cereals like *Shredded Wheat, Weetabix* etc., are most useful for crushing (broken into a strong plastic bag, and crushed with a rolling pin), and can be used instead of breadcrumbs in many dishes, sweet and savoury. For instance, crushed *Weetabix* with a little dark sugar and softened polyunsaturated margarine mixed in, makes a delicious crumble topping to go on any fruit compote to be baked in the oven. *Shredded Wheat* crushed can be used in nutroasts, and whole wheat crispbreads are useful for mixing with softened cheese and herbs for party savoury balls, if made just before serving. Use stale bread to make crumbs for savouries and keep some in a plastic bag in the refrigerator for instant use — they last a few days. Or use stale bread to make croutons for soup, by frying diced bread or, if preferred, whole slices and dicing afterwards, and store as above. Or bake slices of bread in low oven, dice as above, or grate for toasted crumbs.

# 4.

# SOUPS AND STARTERS

## LEEK AND CARROT SOUP
*Serves 4*

**Imperial (Metric)**
2 large carrots
4 leeks
2 oz (55g) polyunsaturated
  margarine
1½ pints (850ml) vegetable stock or
  water
Pinch of sea salt and black pepper
Pinch of nutmeg
2 tablespoonsful chopped parsley

**American**
2 large carrots
4 leeks
5 tablespoonsful polyunsaturated
  margarine
3¾ cupsful vegetable stock or water
Pinch of sea salt and black pepper
Pinch of nutmeg
2 tablespoonsful chopped parsley

1. Wash and finely slice the carrots and leeks. Fry these in the margarine for 10 minutes without browning.

2. Add hot stock or water, and cook very gently for about 30 minutes till tender.

3. Remove a cupful of soup from the pan and set aside. Liquidize the rest of the soup, return the unliquidized cupful (this gives colour and texture).

4. Season to taste with nutmeg, salt and pepper, and add the chopped parsley just before serving.

*Note:* If you haven't a liquidizer, either leave it as a chunky soup, or push soup through a wire sieve over a basin, with a spoon. Add removed cupful, and reheat.

# FRESH TOMATO SOUP *Illustrated in colour.*
*Serves 4*

**Imperial (Metric)**
6 large firm tomatoes
2 oz (55g) polyunsaturated
   margarine
1 small onion
1 bay leaf
2 cloves
2 pints (1.15 litres) hot vegetable
   stock
Pinch of sea salt, black pepper and
   nutmeg
Pinch of basil

**American**
6 large firm tomatoes
5 tablespoonsful polyunsaturated
   margarine
1 small onion
1 bay leaf
2 cloves
5 cupsful hot vegetable stock
Pinch of sea salt, black pepper and
   nutmeg
Pinch of basil

1.  Wash and thinly slice the tomatoes.

2.  Heat margarine and gently fry tomatoes until very soft.

3.  Peel the onion, wrap the bay leaf around it and push the two cloves
    through the leaf into the onion. Add to pan with the hot vegetable
    stock. Simmer gently for about 20 minutes.

4.  Remove onion, bay leaf and cloves, add salt, pepper, nutmeg and
    basil. Liquidize or pass through a sieve over a basin, with a spoon,
    and gently reheat.

*Note:* To serve, garnish with either finely chopped parsley, celery
leaves or watercress leaves floating on top.

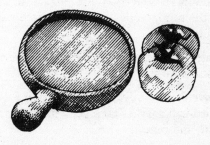

## MINTY GREEN PEA SOUP *Illustrated in colour.*
*Serves 4*

| Imperial (Metric) | American |
|---|---|
| ½ lb (225g) split green peas | 1 cupful split green peas |
| 2 large onions | 2 large onions |
| 2 large carrots | 2 large carrots |
| 2 oz (55g) polyunsaturated margarine | ¼ cupful polyunsaturated margarine |
| 2 pints (1.15 litres) hot vegetable stock | 5 cupsful hot vegetable stock |
| 1 tablespoonful chopped mint leaves | 1 tablespoonful chopped mint leaves |
| 1½ teaspoonsful yeast extract | 1½ teaspoonsful yeast extract |

1.  Wash split peas and soak in about 2 pints (1.15 litres/5 cupsful) of water for 3 hours. Cook in this water in a large saucepan over a low heat until tender, about 50-60 minutes.

2.  When split peas are almost cooked, chop the onions and carrots. Melt margarine in second large pan and add onions and carrots. Cook without browning these for 5 minutes.

3.  Add hot vegetable stock and bring to the boil with lid on, turn down to simmer for 10 minutes.

4.  Drain the cooked peas. Mash well with a potato masher, liquidize, or put through a sieve over a basin, with a spoon.

5.  Add the mashed peas and chopped mint to the pan with the carrots and onions, stir well while reheating. Add yeast extract just before serving, stirring to dissolve it.

# JULIENNE SOUP
*Serves 4*

| **Imperial (Metric)** | **American** |
|---|---|
| 2 large onions | 2 large onions |
| 2 large carrots | 2 large carrots |
| 2 or more sticks of celery | 2 or more stalks of celery |
| 2 small courgettes | 2 small zucchini |
| 2 tablespoonsful vegetable oil | 2 tablespoonsful vegetable oil |
| 1 bay leaf | 1 bay leaf |
| 2 pints (1.15 litres) hot vegetable stock | 5 cupsful hot vegetable stock |
| 2 tablespoonsful tomato *purée* | 2 tablespoonsful tomato paste |
| 1½ teaspoonsful vegetable yeast extract | 1½ teaspoonsful vegetable yeast extract |
| 2 tablespoonsful chopped fresh chives | 2 tablespoonsful chopped fresh chives |

1.  Wash and slice all vegetables and cut into matchstick sized pieces.

2.  Gently heat vegetable oil and fry the vegetables without browning, for about 5 minutes, carefully turning them over occasionally.

3.  Add hot stock and bay leaf. Simmer for about 30 minutes.

4.  When vegetables are tender, remove bay leaf, carefully stir in the yeast extract and tomato *purée*. When serving, sprinkle the chopped chives over the top of the soup.

# FRESH AND TANGY STARTERS *Illustrated in colour.*

- Dessert apple slices or pear slices, sprinkled with orange juice and powdered ginger, cinnamon or cloves.
- Peeled and sliced oranges, banana slices and orange juice, sprinkled with a little cinnamon.
- Juicy William Pears stuffed with softened dates.
- Sliced juicy strawberries layered with sliced cucumber.
- Thinly sliced peeled oranges, tomatoes and onion rings.
- Pineapple ring on top of coarsely grated carrot, and sprigs of watercress.
- Melon portions scattered with fresh redcurrants.
- Grated dessert apple mixed with raw or cooked beetroot (beet) on a base of lettuce, watercress, or cress.
- Fresh grapefruit and orange sections with toasted hazelnuts.
- Grated raw turnip, grated carrot, onion rings, sprinkled with toasted sesame seeds, garnished with parsley.
- Sliced raw mushrooms and tomatoes on shredded lettuce.
- Grated celeriac, chopped tomatoes, garden peas or chick peas (garbanzos), with mint, savory or basil herbs.
- Finely chopped cabbage, red, white or green, with caraway seeds, in an oil and lemon dressing, with strips of red pepper.
- Chopped raw Brussels sprouts and sliced tomatoes with dressing.
- Raw cauliflower florets, carrot and cucumber sticks with dressing.
- *Tartex* or *Granose* vegetable paste with toast squares, melba toast, wholemeal biscuits etc.
- Halved avocado, topped with thin tomato slices and dressing.

# 5.

# SNACKS AND LUNCHES

## HOME-MADE PASTES FOR SPREADING

Simply mash together your chosen ready-grated or chopped
ingredients (see below), along with softened margarine or oil, until
a fairly smooth paste is obtained; taste, adjust seasoning if necessary,
cover with a lid or clingfilm, and place in cold corner or refrigerator
until required — don't leave it there longer than 24 hours. Most of
these spreads can be made overnight for morning-rush spreading!

- A few spoonsful of any kind of left-over beans mashed with
  tomato pulp, tomato *purée* (paste) and herbs of choice.
- Cream cheese, chopped chives and finely chopped raw
  mushrooms.
- Finely grated Cheddar cheese with grated raw or cooked
  beetroot(beet) and grated horseradish.
- Peanut butter with either chopped celery or onion rings; or
  fresh chopped herbs; or mashed banana.
- Cream cheese, chopped pineapple pieces with a little mint.
- Finely grated Cheddar cheese, mashed soaked dates and grated
  orange rind.
- Slices of home-made (or tinned) nutroast (see page 54) with
  chutney.
- Home-made lentil paste (see page 40) with chopped onion.
- *Tartex* paste or *Granose* sandwich spread (from health food
  stores) with any finely ground nuts.

## LENTIL PASTE *Illustrated in colour.*

| Imperial (Metric) | American |
|---|---|
| 4 oz (115g) split red lentils | ½ cupful split red lentils |
| ½ pint (285ml) cold water | 1⅓ cupsful cold water |
| 1 small onion | 1 small onion |
| 1 bay leaf | 1 bay leaf |
| 2 cloves | 2 cloves |
| 1 oz (30g) polyunsaturated margarine | 2½ tablespoonsful polyunsaturated margarine |
| Pinch of nutmeg | Pinch of nutmeg |
| Pinch of sea salt | Pinch of sea salt |
| 1 tablespoonful very finely chopped parsley | 1 tablespoonful very finely chopped parsley |

1.  Pick over lentils and remove any stones; wash lentils in fine sieve and put in saucepan with water.

2.  Peel onion, wrap bay leaf round it, press the two cloves through the leaf into the onion and place in pan.

3.  Put on lid, bring to boil, turn down low to simmer for 15-20 minutes. Water should have been absorbed and lentils be soft and fluffy.

4.  Remove onion (use for soup, without cloves), add all other ingredients and blend with a fork until smooth. Allow to cool and become firm in basin. Cover if keeping in refrigerator.

*Note:* This recipe may also be set in a mould (use double quantity) and is sliceable to go with salad. Curry powder or paste, horseradish powder or grated, fresh or dried herbs, mustard powder or paste, chutney or pickles, are all suitable tasty variations to include — one at a time! Most other cooked split peas, beans, green or brown lentils, and chick peas (garbanzos), can be used, mashed or blended, with ingredients as above to flavour them. See chart on page 23 for how to cook pulses.

## HUMMUS *Illustrated in colour.*
*A starter or a party dip.*

| Imperial (Metric) | American |
|---|---|
| 6 oz (170g) cooked chick peas | 1 cupful cooked garbanzos |
| 2 tablespoonful olive oil | 2 tablespoonsful olive oil |
| 2-3 cloves of garlic, peeled | 2-3 cloves of garlic, peeled |
| 1 dessertspoonful lemon juice | 2 teaspoonsful lemon juice |
| Pinch of sea salt and black pepper | Pinch of sea salt and black pepper |
| 1 tablespoonful sesame paste (Tahini) | 1 tablespoonful sesame paste (Tahini) |
| Paprika pepper and chopped parsley to garnish | Paprika pepper and chopped parsley to garnish |

1. Blend chick peas (garbanzos), oil, garlic, lemon juice, salt and pepper in a liquidizer.

2. Add sesame paste (and a little cold water, if rather thick) and blend till smooth. Spoon into bowl and garnish with paprika pepper and chopped parsley. Serve with bread, melba toast or raw vegetable sticks.

*Note:* Tinned chick peas (garbanzos), drained, can be used, and 2-4 tablespoonsful of natural yogurt instead of sesame paste, for variation. Use a wire sieve and wooden spoon to crush the chick peas (garbanzos) over mixing bowl, if you haven't a liquidizer, and push through the sieve several times before mixing in other ingredients.

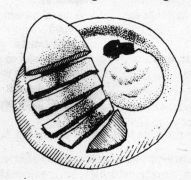

# GUACAMOLE DIP OR SPREAD *Illustrated in colour.*

| Imperial (Metric) | American |
|---|---|
| 1 large ripe avocado | 1 large ripe avocado |
| 1 teaspoonful lemon juice | 1 teaspoonful lemon juice |
| 1 tablespoonful natural yogurt (optional) | 1 tablespoonful natural yogurt (optional) |
| 1 teaspoonful soya sauce | 1 teaspoonful soy sauce |
| 1 small stick of celery | 1 small stalk of celery |
| 1 or 2 spring onions (with tops for garnish) | 1 or 2 scallions (with tops for garnish) |
| Black pepper | Black pepper |
| Pinch of chilli powder | Pinch of chili powder |

1.  Cut avocado in half, remove stone and skin, and chop into pieces in a basin. Add lemon juice and soya sauce and mash with a fork.

2.  Finely chop the celery and onions and add to basin with a little black pepper and chilli (chili) powder. Mix well, spoon into serving bowl, garnish with more black pepper and a little chopped green onion on top.

*Note:* Serve with raw vegetable sticks or on bread.


# HAZELNUT SPREAD

| Imperial (Metric) | American |
|---|---|
| 2 oz (55g) roasted hazelnuts (or other nuts) | ½ cupful roasted hazelnuts (or other nuts) |
| 1 large tomato | 1 large tomato |
| 1 teaspoonful vegetable oil | 1 teaspoonful vegetable oil |
| Pinch of sweet basil | Pinch of sweet basil |
| Pinch of sea salt | Pinch of sea salt |
| Pinch of black pepper | Pinch of black pepper |

1.  Finely grate the nuts and put in to mixing bowl.

2.  Put tomato into boiling water, remove after one minute with a fork or spoon, rinse in cold water and remove skin. Chop tomato on a plate and add to bowl.

3. Add oil, basil, salt and pepper and mix till smooth with a fork.

*Note:* Use to spread on bread or biscuits, or make into large marbles and roll in coarse grated nuts to serve on sticks for parties, or even larger sizes to serve with a salad. For variety, add one teaspoon or more of curry paste instead of herbs. Make a paste as above, spoon into serving dish and garnish with thinly sliced cucumber.

## DATE AND NUT SPREAD

| Imperial (Metric) | American |
| --- | --- |
| 10 oz (285g) dried dates | 2 cupsful dried dates |
| 2 oz (55g) roasted walnuts, peanuts or cashews | ½ cupful roasted English walnuts, peanuts or cashews |
| 2 teaspoonsful grated orange rind | 2 teaspoonsful grated orange rind |
| 1 teaspoonful powdered ginger | 1 teaspoonful powdered ginger |
| ½ pint (285ml) boiling water | 1⅓ cupsful boiling water |

1. Wash and chop the dates, add to mixing bowl with boiling water, leave to soften 1-2 hours.

2. Finely grate the nuts and add to bowl with orange rind and ginger. Mix well with a fork till smooth.

*Note:* Spread on bread or party biscuits. Or the mixture can be put in a pastry case, and topped with sliced apples or pears etc. and baked till fruit is soft.

# GOMA SIO

| Imperial (Metric) | American |
|---|---|
| 6 oz (170g) sesame seeds | 1 cupful sesame seeds |
| 2 level teaspoonsful rock or sea salt crystals | 2 level teaspoonsful rock or sea salt crystals |

1. Roast sesame seeds on a shallow baking tray in oven or under grill at medium heat, stirring occasionally, for about 8 minutes until just golden.

2. Remove a spoonful at a time into a mortar (or china basin). Use a pestle (or metal spoon) to grind seeds to a powder. Transfer to another bowl.

3. When all seeds are ground, grind the salt as well, and mix into the sesame powder. Store in an airtight container and use as a condiment to help reduce salt intake.

## QUICK LUNCHES AT HOME

If you are lunching alone, please try to have one of the following dishes, or similar — don't go without or have an unbalanced meal just because it seems too much bother for one. Over a long period, this can play havoc with your health. These mini-meals are easy to put together and are quite inexpensive.

Some quick ideas . . .

- Grated raw beetroot (beet) mixed with toasted sesame seeds and chopped parsley, piled onto an avocado half and served on a base of lettuce or watercress, with thin tomato slices.
- Tinned celery hearts or steamed broccoli spears, with a mixture of grated cheese, sesame seeds and breadcrumbs spread on top and put under the grill for a few minutes.
- Tinned kidney beans or haricot (navy) beans can be rinsed, drained and mixed with a salad dressing and other salad items such as tomatoes, cucumber, raw mushrooms, herbs and leftover cooked rice, to make a quick protein dish to go with a green salad.

# TOMATO AND MUSHROOM SAVOURY
*Serves 1*

| Imperial (Metric) | American |
|---|---|
| 2 medium tomatoes | 2 medium tomatoes |
| 4 oz (115g) mushrooms | 2 cupsful mushrooms |
| 1 oz (30g) polyunsaturated margarine | 2½ tablespoonsful polyunsaturated margarine |
| A few spring onions | A few scallions |
| Medium slice wholemeal bread | Medium slice wholewheat bread |
| 2 oz (55g) mixed nuts — Brazils and walnuts | ½ cupful mixed nuts — Brazils and English walnuts |
| Pinch of mixed herbs | Pinch of mixed herbs |
| 2 teaspoonsful vegetable oil | 2 teaspoonsful vegetable oil |

1.  Wash and slice the tomatoes and arrange in an oiled ovenproof dish.

2.  Fry the washed and chopped mushrooms in the margarine for 2 minutes only and add to dish.

3.  With scissors, snip the onions over the dish.

4.  Grate the bread and nuts in a mouli-mill, and put in a basin with the herbs and oil, mixing well to bind the mixture. Spread this mixture over the mushrooms and place dish either under a medium grill for 10 minutes or in medium oven for 15 minutes. Garnish with watercress and serve.

# CHEESE AND APPLE TOAST
*Serves 1*

| Imperial (Metric) | American |
|---|---|
| 2 oz (55g) Cheddar cheese | 1/2 cupful Cheddar cheese |
| 1 dessert apple | 1 dessert apple |
| 1 slice of wholemeal bread | 1 slice of wholewheat bread |
| 1 medium tomato | 1 medium tomato |
| Watercress to serve | Watercress to serve |

1. Grate the cheese and the unpeeled but cored apple and mix together in a basin.

2. Toast one side of bread, turn over and spoon on cheese mixture. Grill until melted.

3. Slice the tomato and arrange across the toast, and garnish with watercress.


# LENTIL PASTE WITH MUSHROOMS ON TOAST
*Serves 1*

| Imperial (Metric) | American |
|---|---|
| 1 slice of wholemeal bread | 1 slice of wholewheat bread |
| 2 oz (55g) lentil paste (page 40) | 1/3 cupful lentil paste (page 40) |
| 2 spring onions | 2 scallions |
| 2 oz (55g) mushrooms | 1 cupful mushrooms |
| 2 teaspoonsful polyunsaturated margarine | 2 teaspoonsful polyunsaturated margarine |
| Cress and cucumber to serve | Cress and cucumber to serve |

1. Toast one side of the bread and spread with lentil paste.

2. With scissors, snip the onions over the paste.

3. Sprinkle washed and chopped mushrooms over the paste.

4.  Spread the margarine over the mushrooms with a palette knife and grill gently for 5 minutes.

5.  Garnish with cress and cucumber slices.


# SPAGHETTI NEAPOLITAN
*Serves 1*

| Imperial (Metric) | American |
|---|---|
| 2 oz (55g) wholemeal spaghetti | 2 ounces wholewheat spaghetti |
| ¾ pint (425ml) water | 2 cupsful water |
| 2 tablespoonsful vegetable oil | 2 tablespoonsful vegetable oil |
| 1 small onion | 1 small onion |
| Small piece of green or red pepper | Small piece of green or red pepper |
| 2 medium tomatoes and ¼ pint (140ml) water *or* | 2 medium tomatoes and ⅔ cupful water *or* |
| 1 small tin of tomatoes with juice | 1 small can of tomatoes with juice |
| Pinch of oregano and sea salt | Pinch of oregano and sea salt |
| 2 oz (55g) grated Cheddar cheese or nuts | ½ cupful grated Cheddar cheese or nuts |
| Green salad to serve | Green salad to serve |

1.  Bring water to boil in saucepan, add one teaspoonful of the oil, a pinch of salt, and the spaghetti (gently lower this into the water as it softens). Boil for about 8 minutes.

2.  Meanwhile, chop the onion and green pepper and gently fry in rest of oil for 5 minutes, add chopped tomatoes and water (or juice) and oregano. Stir well, and mash the tomatoes with a potato masher. Keep hot.

3.  Drain spaghetti in a fine sieve, and spoon onto a warmed plate. Pour on hot sauce, top with cheese or chopped nuts, and serve the green salad on a side plate.

# WELSH RAREBIT SPECIAL
*Serves 1*

| Imperial (Metric) | American |
|---|---|
| 2 tablespoonsful milk | 2 tablespoonsful milk |
| ½ level teaspoonful mustard powder (or more) | ½ level teaspoonful mustard powder (or more) |
| 2 oz (55g) grated Cheddar cheese | ½ cupful grated Cheddar cheese |
| 1 medium tomato | 1 medium tomato |
| 1 slice wholemeal bread | 1 slice wholewheat bread |
| A few chives or spring onions | A few chives or scallions |
| Lettuce or chicory to serve | Lettuce or chicory to serve |

1.  Put the milk, mustard powder and cheese in a saucepan over a low heat, and stir all the time until melted. Add chopped tomatoes, chopped chives and stir again.

2.  Toast the bread, put on a plate and spoon on the cheese mixture. Arrange the lettuce or chicory on the dish.

# NUTTY FRIES
*Serves 1*

| Imperial (Metric) | American |
| --- | --- |
| 1 medium tomato | 1 medium tomato |
| 2 rounded tablespoonsful of Savormix or Frittamix | 2 rounded tablespoonsful of Savormix or Frittamix |
| 1 dessertspoonful of sesame seeds or grated nuts | 2 teaspoonsful of sesame seeds or grated nuts |
| Pinch of mixed herbs | Pinch of mixed herbs |
| 2 teaspoonsful finely chopped onion | 2 teaspoonsful finely chopped onion |
| 1 level teaspoonful vegetable yeast extract | 1 level teaspoonful vegetable yeast extract |
| 2 dessertspoonsful boiling water | 4 teaspoonsful boiling water |
| 1 tablespoonful wholemeal flour for coating | 1 tablespoonful wholewheat flour for coating |
| Oil for frying | Oil for frying |

1. Wash and chop the tomato. Put in a mixing bowl.

2. Add *Savormix*, sesame seeds, herbs and onion to the bowl and mix well.

3. Dissolve yeast extract in boiling water in a cup, stir well, and add to mixture in bowl. Mix well and leave to cool.

4. With floured hands, form large tablespoonsful of mixture into ½ in. (1cm) thick flat rounds, or triangular shapes. Coat in flour on a plate, and fry in hot oil on both sides, till golden.

*Note: Savormix* or *Frittamix* are nut and cereal mixtures, available at health food stores. Sunflower or pumpkin seeds, chopped celery, green pepper, mushrooms, or diced cooked beetroot can be used to vary the mixture.

# PAN HAGGERTY
*Serves 1*

| Imperial (Metric) | American |
| --- | --- |
| 1 medium potato (scrub well, leave skin on) | 1 medium potato (scrub well, leave skin on) |
| 1 small onion | 1 small onion |
| 2 oz (55g) polyunsaturated margarine | 5 tablespoonsful polyunsaturated margarine |
| 2 heaped tablespoonsful grated cheese | 2 heaped tablespoonsful grated cheese |
| Pinch of sea salt and black pepper | Pinch of sea salt and black pepper |

1.  Thinly slice the potato and onion into rings.

2.  Gently heat margarine in a shallow frying pan (skillet). Put in a layer of potatoes, then a layer of onion rings, topped by half the grated cheese. Continue with another layer of each item, and sprinkle with salt and pepper.

3.  Fry very gently with a lid or a large plate over the pan, for about 25 minutes. Test with fork for tenderness. If ready, turn carefully with a food slice, *or* put under medium grill, still in the pan with lid removed, for 2-3 minutes, to brown.

4.  Slice or lift onto plate, and garnish with watercress chopped celery and tomatoes.

*Note:* Short cut. Boil the potato whole for 6-7 minutes first, then slice and proceed as above, with a 15 minute cooking time. Instead of cheese, try a small tin of curried beans, as a layer.

# CHINESE STIR-FRY
*Serves 1*

| Imperial (Metric) | American |
|---|---|
| 1 small onion | 1 small onion |
| 4 medium mushrooms | 4 medium mushrooms |
| Piece of green pepper | Piece of green pepper |
| 1 large stick of celery | 1 large stalk of celery |
| 1 medium tomato | 1 medium tomato |
| Small chunk of white cabbage | Small chunk of white cabbage |
| 1 small carrot | 1 small carrot |
| 2 tablespoonsful vegetable oil | 2 tablespoonsful vegetable oil |
| Pinch of sea salt and black pepper | Pinch of sea salt and black pepper |
| 1 dessertspoonful soya sauce | 2 teaspoonsful soy sauce |
| ¼ pint (140ml) hot water | ⅔ cupful hot water |
| 2 oz (55g) flaked almonds | ½ cupful slivered almonds |
| 2 teaspoonsful chopped parsley | 2 teaspoonsful chopped parsley |

1. Thinly slice the onion into rings. Slice the mushrooms and green pepper thinly. Chop the celery, tomato and cabbage small. Grate the carrot, and set all aside on a large plate.

2. Heat the oil in a large frying pan or wok, and gradually add the vegetables, starting with the carrot, then onion, cabbage and celery, followed by the green pepper, mushrooms and tomato.

3. Keep turning the vegetables over gently with a food slice, add salt, pepper, soya sauce and hot water. Keep the vegetables moving gently for up to 5 minutes only. Add the almonds and parsley and serve.

*Note:* Beansprouts can be added too, either home-grown or bought, and the dish is usually served with boiled rice.

# MUESLI

A meal in itself, if made with plenty of fresh fruit and grated nuts (see page 29). No cooking, and only one bowl, spoon, and knife or grater to wash up!

Muesli is delicious to eat at any time of day, and is quick to make if you are in a hurry. If you usually soak the oats or cereal mixture overnight, then a quick way to soften them instead, is to use hot liquid (milk or water perhaps), allow a few minutes to soak, then add more liquid, fruit and grated nuts etc., as usual.

# FRUIT, NUT AND MILK SHAKE
*Serves 1*

| Imperial (Metric) | American |
|---|---|
| 4 oz (115g) fresh fruit — strawberries, raspberries, peaches, apricots, etc. | 1 cupful fresh fruit — strawberries, raspberries, peaches, apricots, etc. |
| 1 oz (30g) powdered nuts — almonds, cashews, hazelnuts, etc. | ¼ cupful powdered nuts — almonds, cashews, hazelnuts, etc. |
| ¼ pint (140ml) milk, diluted *Plamil* or *Granose* soyamilk | ⅔ cupful milk, diluted *Plamil* or *Granose* soyamilk |
| 1 teaspoonful Demerara sugar | 1 teaspoonful Demerara sugar |
| Few drops vanilla essence | Few drops vanilla essence |

Put washed and chopped fruit and all other ingredients into an electric blender or food processor, and blend till smooth.

*OR*

Push chopped fruit through a wire sieve over a bowl, with a spoon, and mix in other ingredients thoroughly.

*Note:* Sip very slowly through a straw. Use fresh, tinned and drained fruit of choice (choose fruit tinned in its own juice or apple juice, if you can), or use thawed and lightly cooked fruit from your freezer.

# PACKED LUNCHES

For school, workplace, travelling or picnics.

May I suggest that you pack a salad separately in a polythene bag or plastic box — with a mini-fork — as most salad items spoil very quickly between slices of bread.

Try scrubbed carrot sticks, crisp raw cauliflower florets, lettuce hearts, small firm tomatoes, spring onions (scallions), chunky sticks of green pepper, celery, endive or chicory, cucumber or radishes. By simply washing any of these items quickly in the morning and popping them in the bag or box, instead of shredding or chopping them, you will be helping to conserve the vitamins therein. Always prepare salad items that are to be shredded or finely chopped just before you are going to eat them. Please do not leave any kind of greenery or vegetables, be they for salad or cooking, soaking in water for long periods before use; you could be leaving vital elements behind in the water. Take a wholemeal sandwich or roll to eat with your salad, filled with one of the many suggestions on pages 39-43. They are easy to make, and all you need are a small china bowl, a fork, spoon and small wire sieve.

To complete your meal, take a piece of fresh fruit — apple, pear, orange, etc. or a wrapped Fruit and Nut Bar (page 90). These bars can be individually wrapped in clingfilm, and stored in a tin in a cool place for about two weeks, if necessary.

# 6.

# YOUR EVENING MEAL

Here is a selection of savouries and composite meals, to be served with either a salad or fresh short-cooked vegetables, always including a green one.

## SESAME AND BRAZIL NUT ROAST
*Serves 4*

| Imperial (Metric) | American |
|---|---|
| 6 oz (170g) raw or roasted Brazil nuts | 1⅓ cupsful raw or roasted Brazil nuts |
| 2 oz (55g) sesame seeds | ⅓ cupful sesame seeds |
| 3 oz (85g) fresh wholemeal breadcrumbs | 1½ cupsful fresh wholewheat breadcrumbs |
| 1 oz (30g) rolled oats | ¼ cupful rolled oats |
| 1 teaspoonful dried herbs or 1 tablespoonful fresh chopped herbs | 1 teaspoonful dried herbs or 1 tablespoonful fresh chopped herbs |
| 2 large tomatoes | 2 large tomatoes |
| 1 rounded teaspoonful vegetable yeast extract | 1 rounded teaspoonful vegetable yeast extract |
| ¼ pint (140ml) vegetable stock or water and stock cube | ⅔ cupful vegetable stock or water and stock cube |
| 1 large onion | 1 large onion |
| 2 dessertspoonsful vegetable oil | 4 teaspoonsful vegetable oil |
| 1 oz (30g) plain wholemeal flour | ¼ cupful plain wholewheat flour |

1. Grate the Brazil nuts into a large mixing bowl, add the sesame seeds, breadcrumbs, oats and herbs. Chop tomatoes and add to bowl.

2. Put yeast extract into hot stock to dissolve, stir well, set aside.

3. Chop the onion and fry gently in the oil in a saucepan. After 5 minutes, stir in the flour so that it is absorbed by the oil. Carefully stir in the hot stock and simmer whilst stirring until sauce has thickened — about 3 minutes.

4. Add this sauce to the mixing bowl, and mix well.

5. Oil a 1 lb (500g) loaf tin or deep ovenproof dish, and spoon in the mixture. Smooth top and bake in oven 30-40 minutes at 375°F/190°C (Gas Mark 5).

*Note:* When the Nut Roast is cooked, i.e. firm and becoming brown on top, it can be removed from the loaf tin, by sliding a knife around all sides, placing a small flat baking tray over the tin, and inverting the tin onto the tray. If any mixture remains in the tin, do not despair, scrape it with a spoon and repair the loaf carefully, brush with oil (or spread with a little margarine) and return to the oven for 5-7 minutes. This will give a nice crunchy outside texture, and the loaf can be lifted onto a serving dish, and garnished with tomato slices and chopped parsley, and surrounded with sprigs of watercress.

At Christmas time, the loaf could be decorated with holly leaves cut from green peppers, and 'berries' from red pepper or tomato! (See page 32 for a Rich Brown Sauce to serve with Nut Roast.)

# GOLDEN SLICE
*Serves 4*

| Imperial (Metric) | American |
|---|---|
| 1 rounded teaspoonful soya flour | 1 rounded teaspoonful soy flour |
| 4 tablespoonsful milk or water | 4 tablespoonsful milk or water |
| 6 oz (170g) Cheddar cheese | 1½ cupsful Cheddar cheese |
| 2 large carrots | 2 large carrots |
| 2 oz (55g) polyunsaturated margarine | 5 tablespoonsful polyunsaturated margarine |
| 5 oz (140g) rolled oats | 1¼ cupsful rolled oats |
| Pinch of sea salt and black pepper | Pinch of sea salt and black pepper |
| Pinch of thyme or mixed herbs | Pinch of thyme or mixed herbs |
| ½ level teaspoonful celery seed | ½ level teaspoonful celery seed |

1. Mix the soya flour with the milk in a small basin until smooth.

2. Grate the cheese and carrots and set aside on a plate.

3. Melt the margarine in a large pan, remove from heat, and stir in the cheese and carrots, oats, soya flour mixture, salt, pepper, thyme and celery seed, and mix well. If it seems rather stiff, add a little more milk or water and mix again.

4. Oil an ovenproof dish, spoon in mixture and smooth the top evenly. Bake for 25 minutes at 375°F/190°C (Gas Mark 5). Garnish with sprigs of parsley.

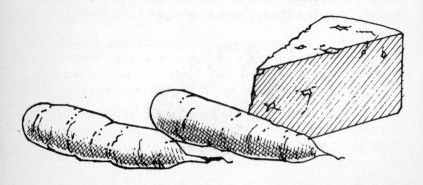

# FRUITY BLACK-EYE BEANS *Illustrated in colour.*
*Serves 4*

| Imperial (Metric) | American |
|---|---|
| ½ lb (225g) black-eye beans | 1 cupful black-eye beans |
| Pinch of sea salt | Pinch of sea salt |
| 1 medium onion | 1 medium onion |
| 2 medium apples (dessert or cooking) | 2 medium apples (dessert or cooking) |
| 2 tablespoonful raisins | 2 tablespoonful raisins |
| Small tin of pineapple rings, or fresh pineapple | Small can of pineapple rings, or fresh pineapple |
| 2 teaspoonful molasses | 2 teaspoonful molasses |
| ½ pint (285ml) water or pineapple juice | 1⅓ cupful water or pineapple juice |

1. Cover unsoaked beans with plenty of water in large saucepan, bring to boil, put on lid, turn down to simmer till tender (about 30 minutes). Add a pinch of salt near end of cooking time. Drain and set aside.

2. Chop the onion and the unpeeled but cored apples.

3. Chop the pineapple into small pieces. Save the juice.

4. Mix the molasses with any pineapple juice available, or with water to make up to ½ pint.

5. In a large mixing bowl, put the cooked beans, onion, apple, raisins, pineapple and molasses liquid. Mix well.

6. Oil a large, deep ovenproof dish, and spoon in mixture and juice. Cover with a lid or foil and bake in oven at 375°F/190°C (Gas Mark 5) for about 30 minutes. This dish is meant to be sweet and crunchy! Serve with boiled rice and green salad.

*Note:* Haricot (navy) beans or flageolet beans could also be used for this dish, see page 24 for how to cook them. Or use a tin of cannellini beans and proceed from Step 2.

# ADUKI BURGERS
*Serves 2 or 3*

| Imperial (Metric) | American |
|---|---|
| 4 oz (115g) aduki beans | ½ cupful aduki beans |
| 1 pint (570ml) water | 2½ cupsful water |
| Pinch of sea salt | Pinch of sea salt |
| 1 small onion | 1 small onion |
| 1 stick of celery | 1 stalk of celery |
| Piece of green pepper (optional) | Piece of green pepper (optional) |
| 2 oz (55g) mushrooms | 1 cupful mushrooms |
| 2 oz (55g) polyunsaturated margarine | ¼ cupful polyunsaturated margarine |
| 4 oz (115g) rolled oats | 1 cupful rolled oats |
| 1 tablespoonful soya sauce | 1 tablespoonful soy sauce |
| Pinch of dried herbs | Pinch of dried herbs |
| 1 teaspoonful lemon juice | 1 teaspoonful lemon juice |
| 1 tablespoonful finely chopped parsley | 1 tablespoonful finely chopped parsley |
| Wholemeal flour for coating | Wholewheat flour for coating |
| Vegetable oil for frying | Vegetable oil for frying |

1. Soak aduki beans in plenty of water for 3 hours. Drain, add to a large saucepan with 1 pint of water. Bring to the boil, turn down to simmer with a lid on, for 1 hour or until tender. Drain and set aside in large mixing bowl.

2. Chop the onion, celery, pepper and mushrooms fairly small, and fry in heated margarine until softened. Add to the beans in the bowl.

3. Add the oats, soya sauce, herbs, lemon juice and parsley and mix well together with a fork. With floured hands take a heaped table-spoonful of mixture and shape into flat rounds ½ in. (1cm) thick, and dip both sides in flour.

4. Fry in vegetable oil till golden brown on both sides.

*Note:* Fresh wholemeal breadcrumbs may be used instead of oats, or use half and half. Serve with mashed potatoes, chutney and a green vegetable or salad.

## CHEESE AND RICE CROQUETTES
*Serves 2*

| Imperial (Metric) | American |
| --- | --- |
| 3 oz (85g) cooked brown rice | ½ cupful cooked brown rice |
| 1 small onion | 1 small onion |
| ½ to 1 teaspoonful curry powder, to taste | ½ to 1 teaspoonful curry powder, to taste |
| 2 teaspoonsful vegetable oil | 2 teaspoonsful vegetable oil |
| Pinch of sea salt and black pepper | Pinch of sea salt and black pepper |
| 3 oz (85g) grated cheese | ¾ cupful grated cheese |
| 2 tablespoonsful toasted wholemeal breadcrumbs | 2 tablespoonsful toasted wholewheat breadcrumbs |

1. Heat the oil in a frying pan (skillet), add curry powder and chopped onion. Fry gently.

2. Put the cooked rice, grated cheese, salt and pepper in a mixing bowl, add the fried onion and residue oil. Mix well. Allow to cool.

3. With floured hands, shape a heaped tablespoonful of mixture into a cylinder shape by squeezing the mixture hard, and roll each in the toasted breadcrumbs on a plate (see page 33).

5. Place croquettes on an oiled baking tray and bake at 400°F/200°C (Gas Mark 6) for 25 minutes, turning them over half way through the cooking time.

# MACARONI CHEESE SPECIAL
*Serves 4*

| Imperial (Metric) | American |
|---|---|
| 6 large tomatoes | 6 large tomatoes |
| ½ pint (285ml) water | 1⅓ cupsful water |
| Pinch of sea salt and black pepper | Pinch of sea salt and black pepper |
| 2 bay leaves | 2 bay leaves |
| ½ lb (225g) wholemeal macaroni | 2 cupsful wholewheat macaroni |
| 1 large onion | 1 large onion |
| 1-2 cloves of garlic (optional) | 1-2 cloves of garlic (optional) |
| 1 small green pepper | 1 small green pepper |
| 4 oz (115g) mushrooms | 2 cupsful mushrooms |
| 2 oz (55g) polyunsaturated margarine | ¼ cupful polyunsaturated margarine |
| 1 small tin of sweet corn niblets | 1 small can of sweet corn niblets |
| 6 oz (170g) Cheddar cheese | 1½ cupsful Cheddar cheese |
| 1 oz (30g) flaked almonds | ¼ cupful slivered almonds |
| 1 tablespoonful chopped parsley | 1 tablespoonful chopped parsley |

1.  Chop the tomatoes small and put them in a saucepan with the water, salt, pepper and bay leaves. Stir and allow to simmer gently over low heat.

2.  In a large saucepan, bring plenty of water to the boil, add the macaroni and a pinch of salt, and cook for 10-12 minutes, with the lid on, bubbling well. When ready, drain well in a sieve, cover and set aside.

3.  Chop the onion, garlic (if used), pepper and mushrooms and fry gently in the margarine. Open and drain the tin of corn. Set aside.

4.  Oil a large deep ovenproof dish, and add half the drained macaroni. Remove the bay leaves from the tomato sauce, and spoon half of it over the macaroni. Spoon on the corn, and half the cheese.

5.  Tip the rest of the drained macaroni into the fried vegetables, mix well and add to dish. Add the rest of the tomato sauce, grated cheese and the flaked almonds sprinkled on top. Bake at

350°F/180°C (Gas Mark 4) for 20-25 minutes. When ready, sprinkle on the parsley and serve with a green vegetable or salad.

*Note:* You could use a medium tin of tomatoes instead of fresh tomatoes.


# CHICK PEA CROQUETTES
*Serves 2 or 3*

| Imperial (Metric) | American |
|---|---|
| ½ lb (225g) cooked chick peas | 1 cupful cooked garbanzos |
| 1 small onion | 1 small onion |
| 1-2 cloves of garlic (optional) | 1-2 cloves of garlic (optional) |
| 2 tablespoonsful chopped parsley | 2 tablespoonsful chopped parsley |
| 1 medium potato, cooked | 1 medium potato, cooked |
| 1 tablespoonful soya sauce | 1 tablespoonful soy sauce |
| Squeeze of lemon juice | Squeeze of lemon juice |
| Pinch of sea salt and black pepper | Pinch of sea salt and black pepper |
| Flour for coating | Flour for coating |
| Vegetable oil for frying | Vegetable oil for frying |

1. Mash the chick peas (garbanzos) with a potato masher in a large mixing bowl, or push through a sieve, over a basin, with a spoon.

2. Finely chop the onion and garlic (if used), mash the potato, and add to the bowl with the parsley.

3. Add the soy sauce, lemon juice, salt and black pepper and mix well.

4. With floured hands, shape a heaped tablespoonful into a cylinder shape and roll each one in flour to coat. Leave to firm in the refrigerator for an hour if possible.

5. Gently fry in oil, carefully turning to brown all sides.

*Note:* A 14 ounce (400g) tin of chick peas (garbanzos), when drained of water yields about 8 ounces (225g). If you have a food processor, simply put all ingredients except flour and oil into bowl and blend, then proceed as above with Step 4.

# ALMOND AND POTATO LOAF
*Serves 4*

| Imperial (Metric) | American |
|---|---|
| 1 large onion | 1 large onion |
| 2 oz (55g) polyunsaturated margarine | 5 tablespoonsful polyunsaturated margarine |
| ½ lb (225g) blanched and skinned almonds (page 27) | 2 cupsful blanched and skinned almonds (page 27) |
| 4 oz (115g) mushrooms | 2 cupsful mushrooms |
| 2 large tomatoes | 2 large tomatoes |
| ½ teaspoonful tarragon | ½ teaspoonful tarragon |
| 4 medium potatoes, half-cooked, with skins left on | 4 medium potatoes, half-cooked, with skins left on |

1.  Chop the onion and fry gently in heated margarine. Slice the nuts and mushrooms thinly and add to pan, stir for 1 minute only. Put in a large mixing bowl. Chop the tomatoes and add, with the tarragon.

2.  Coarsely grate the potatoes and tip into the bowl. Mix well.

3.  Oil a large loaf tin or deep ovenproof dish, spoon in mixture, pressing down well. Spread a little extra margarine on top. Bake at 375°F/190°C (Gas Mark 5) for about 45 minutes.

*Note:* Other nuts or herbs could be used, as well as tinned tomatoes instead of fresh. Serve with Beetroot (beet) and Apple Salad (page 79), and watercress.

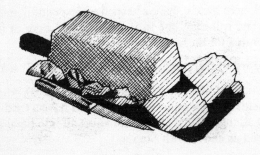

# RATATOUILLE
*Serves 4*

| Imperial (Metric) | American |
|---|---|
| 1 large aubergine | 1 large eggplant |
| 2 large peppers, green and red | 2 large peppers, green and red |
| 2 large onions | 2 large onions |
| 5 large tomatoes | 5 large tomatoes |
| 1 small marrow, *or* | 1 small squash, *or* |
|    4 courgettes |    4 zucchini |
| 1-2 cloves of garlic | 1-2 cloves of garlic |
| 6 tablespoonsful vegetable oil (olive | 6 tablespoonsful vegetable oil (olive |
|    is usual for this dish) |    is usual for this dish) |
| Pinch of sea salt and black pepper | Pinch of sea salt and black pepper |
| 2 tablespoonsful chopped parsley | 2 tablespoonsful chopped parsley |

1.  Slice the aubergine (eggplant) in half, sprinkle cut surfaces with salt, leave for 30 minutes, then rinse away salt and any bitter juice under running water. Skin the tomatoes (page 27). Peel and slice the garlic, and slice all the vegetables into 1 in. (2cm) wide strips or chunks.

2.  Heat the oil, add the vegetables, stir carefully, add salt and pepper, put a lid on the pan and cook over very low heat for about 30 minutes, or until all vegetables are tender, but do not overcook into a mush!

*Note:* Makes a meal when served with wholemeal bread and cheese, and is delicious eaten either hot or cold.

# LENTIL AND TOMATO BAKE
*Serves 4*

| Imperial (Metric) | American |
|---|---|
| 2 large carrots | 2 large carrots |
| 6 large tomatoes | 6 large tomatoes |
| ½ lb (225g) split red lentils | 1 cupful split red lentils |
| 1 small onion | 1 small onion |
| 1 bay leaf | 1 bay leaf |
| 2 cloves | 2 cloves |
| ½ level teaspoonful of mace | ½ level teaspoonful of mace |
| ½ level teaspoonful sea salt | ½ level teaspoonful sea salt |
| 2 oz (55g) polyunsaturated margarine | ¼ cupful polyunsaturated margarine |
| 2 tablespoonsful chopped parsley | 2 tablespoonsful chopped parsley |

1.  Grate carrots, chop tomatoes and set aside.

2.  Remove any small stones from the lentils, wash in sieve under running water, add to a large saucepan with ¾ pint (425ml/2 cupsful) water.

3.  Wrap the bay leaf around the onion, and push the two cloves through the leaf into the onion. Add to pan with the carrots and tomatoes. Bring to the boil, stirring, turn down to simmer, put on the lid, and leave for about 20-25 minutes.

4.  Remove the onion with a spoon (use for soup, without the cloves). Add mace, salt, margarine (save a little to go on top), and parsley. Stir in well.

5.  Spoon into a large ovenproof dish, dot the top with the reserved margarine, and bake at 375°F/190°C (Gas Mark 5) for about 30 minutes.

*Note:* A 14 ounce (400g) tin of tomatoes may be used instead of fresh tomatoes. Use the juice in place of some of the cooking water.

*In order of sequence:*
5.  Cashew and Mushroom Curry (page 72).
6.  Fresh Tomato Soup (page 35) and Minty Green Pea Soup (page 36).
7.  Fruit Jelly (page 86).
8.  Fruity Black-eyed Beans (page 57).

# HUNGARIAN BEAN LOAF
*Serves 4*

| Imperial (Metric) | American |
|---|---|
| ½ lb (225g) cooked butter beans (see page 23) | 1⅓ cupsful cooked Lima beans (see page 23) |
| 1 green pepper | 1 green pepper |
| 1 large onion | 1 large onion |
| 1-2 cloves of garlic (optional) | 1-2 cloves of garlic (optional) |
| 2 tablespoonsful vegetable oil | 2 tablespoonsful vegetable oil |
| ½ level teaspoonful sea salt | ½ level teaspoonful sea salt |
| 1 level teaspoonful paprika | 1 level teaspoonful paprika |
| Pinch of cayenne pepper | Pinch of cayenne pepper |
| 2 tablespoonsful chopped parsley | 2 tablespoonsful chopped parsley |

1. Mash the cooked butter (Lima) beans with a potato masher in a large mixing bowl.

2. Chop the pepper and onion fairly small, slice the garlic (if used), and fry gently in the oil. Add to the bowl (with any remaining oil), and the salt, paprika, cayenne (beware — very hot!) and parsley, and mix all well together.

3. Oil a 1 pound (500g) loaf tin, and spoon mixture in, smooth the top, and bake at 375°F/190°C (Gas Mark 5) for about 35 minutes. When ready, run a knife around edges of loaf and turn out carefully onto a serving dish. Garnish with slices of tomato and lemon twists. (Cut a thin slice of lemon, cut into centre once, turn opposite edges outwards.)

*Note:* Use 2×15 ounce (425g) drained tins of butter (Lima) beans if in a hurry!

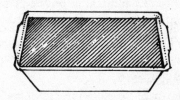

# MUSHROOM PIZZA
*Serves 4*

| Imperial (Metric) | American |
| --- | --- |
| ½ lb (225g) plain wholemeal flour | 2 cupsful plain wholewheat flour |
| 2 teaspoonsful baking powder | 2 teaspoonsful baking soda |
| A little over ¼ pint (140ml) milk | A little over ⅔ cupful milk |
| 2 large onions | 2 large onions |
| 2 tablespoonsful vegetable oil | 2 tablespoonsful vegetable oil |
| 2 extra teaspoonsful wholemeal flour | 2 extra teaspoonsful wholewheat flour |
| ¼ pint (140ml) hot vegetable stock | ⅔ cupful hot vegetable stock |
| 6 large tomatoes | 6 large tomatoes |
| ½ lb (225g) grated cheese | 2 cupsful grated cheese |
| 4 oz (115g) mushrooms | 2 cupsful mushrooms |
| Pinch each of oregano and black pepper | Pinch each of oregano and black pepper |

1. Mix flour and baking powder together in a mixing bowl. Make a well in the centre, pour in some of the milk and mix to a soft dough with a fork, only adding more milk if very crumbly.

2. Brush a 9 × 9 in. (23 × 23cm) baking tin with 1½ in. (4cm) sides, with oil, and press in the dough, flattening it up to the edges.

3. Slice the onions and fry in the oil gently for 3 minutes only, add the extra flour, mix well, and carefully add the hot stock, stirring all the time. Simmer a few minutes to thicken.

4. Chop the tomatoes small and add to the pan with 2 tablespoonsful of the grated cheese and the black pepper. Stir gently and pour onto the dough in baking tin.

5. Chop the mushrooms and scatter on the pizza, add the rest of the cheese on top and sprinkle on oregano. Bake at 400°F/200°C (Gas Mark 6) for about 25 minutes.

*Note:* When making this with a 14 ounce (400g) tin of tomatoes, use the juice instead of hot stock.

# STUFFED VEGETABLES

Many vegetables and fruits can be vessels for a savoury stuffing, to be baked slowly in the oven. Here are just a few — cooked beetroots (beets); large tomatoes; green or red peppers; large onions (cook in boiling water first, then scoop out middle to use in soup, and fill the hollow; aubergines (eggplants); large apples or pears; small cabbages (proceed as with onions); courgettes (zucchini); marrow (squash) (whole, or in 2 in./5cm thick rings); large mushrooms; cooked potatoes etc. Some need to have the top sliced off, such as tomatoes (remove pulp and mix into stuffing), and peppers (remember to remove the seeds and discard, and partly cook in boiling water first). Use the tops as lids, if you like. Aubergines (eggplants), courgettes (zucchini) and cooked potatoes, can be halved lengthways, and the filling pressed down firmly on top, and baked. Use an apple corer or teaspoon to scoop out centres of beetroots (beets), apples and pears and use for salad.

Each stuffing mix is enough for two large vegetables.


## STUFFING I *Illustrated in colour.*

| Imperial (Metric) | American |
|---|---|
| 2 heaped tablespoonsful wholemeal breadcrumbs | 2 heaped tablespoonsful wholewheat breadcrumbs |
| 2 heaped tablespoonsful grated mixed nuts (raw or roasted) | 2 heaped tablespoonsful grated mixed nuts (raw or roasted) |
| 1 tablespoonful finely chopped parsley | 1 tablespoonful finely chopped parsley |
| 1 tablespoonful soya sauce | 1 tablespoonful soy sauce |
| Pinch of black pepper | Pinch of black pepper |
| 3 finely chopped spring onions | 3 finely chopped scallions |

Mix all together in a basin, adding a little hot water or stock to bind if necessary.

# STUFFING II *Illustrated in colour.*

**Imperial (Metric)**
2 heaped tablespoonsful cooked
   brown rice
2 heaped tablespoonsful cooked
   beans (any kind)
1 tablespoonful chopped fresh mint
Pinch of thyme
Pinch of marjoram
1 small finely grated onion mixed
   with a teaspoonful of
   polyunsaturated margarine
Pinch of black pepper

**American**
2 heaped tablespoonsful cooked
   brown rice
2 heaped tablespoonsful cooked
   beans (any kind)
1 tablespoonful chopped fresh mint
Pinch of thyme
Pinch of marjoram
1 small finely grated onion mixed
   with a teaspoonful of
   polyunsaturated margarine
Pinch of black pepper

Mix as Stuffing I.

## STUFFING III *Illustrated in colour.*

**Imperial (Metric)**
2 heaped tablespoonsful of cooked
  brown rice
2 tablespoonsful of chopped walnuts
1 teaspoonful (or more, to taste)
  curry paste
1 tablespoonful raisins
1 small chopped apple
Coconut for garnish

**American**
2 heaped tablespoonsful of cooked
  brown rice
2 tablespoonsful of chopped English
  walnuts
1 teaspoonful (or more, to taste)
  curry paste
1 tablespoonful raisins
1 small chopped apple
Coconut for garnish

1. Soak raisins in water or orange juice for 1 hour before use, if possible.

2. Mix all ingredients (except coconut) together in a bowl, using a little of the juice or water, if needed, to bind together.

3. After baking, garnish with either shredded coconut or desiccated coconut.

*Note:* Brush all stuffed vegetables with oil and put into an oiled ovenproof dish, cover with lid or foil. Test vegetables with a sharp knife to see if they are tender after 30 minutes at 375°F/190°C (Gas Mark 5).

If you want the stuffing to be crisp and golden on top, remove the lid or foil and return dish to the oven for a few minutes.

# CHEESE, APPLE AND BEETROOT FLAN
*Serves 4*

| Imperial (Metric) | American |
|---|---|
| ½ lb (225g) wholemeal pastry (see page 28) | 8 ounces wholewheat pastry (see page 28) |
| ½ lb (225g) Cheddar cheese | 2 cupsful Cheddar cheese |
| 1 large apple (cooking or dessert) | 1 large apple (cooking or dessert) |
| 1 large cooked, peeled beetroot | 1 large cooked, peeled beet |
| 1 rounded teaspoonful ground coriander (or crushed coriander seeds) | 1 rounded teaspoonful ground coriander (or crushed coriander seeds) |
| ½ teaspoonful celery seed | ½ teaspoonful celery seed |

1. Line an 8 in. (20cm) ovenproof flan dish with the pastry.

2. Grate the cheese, apple and beetroot into a large mixing bowl. Add coriander and celery seed and mix well.

3. Spoon this mixture into the flan dish, press down gently. Bake at 375°F/190°C (Gas Mark 5) for 25-30 minutes.

*Note:* Garnish with chopped parsley, and serve with creamed or jacket potatoes and chopped spring greens.

# CHICK PEAS WITH RICE
*Serves 4*

| Imperial (Metric) | American |
|---|---|
| ½ lb (225g) brown rice | 1 cupful brown rice |
| 1 large onion | 1 large onion |
| 3 tablespoonsful vegetable oil | 3 tablespoonsful vegetable oil |
| 1 pint (570ml) hot vegetable stock | 2½ cupsful hot vegetable stock |
| Pinch of sea salt | Pinch of sea salt |
| 4 large tomatoes | 4 large tomatoes |
| 2 courgettes | 2 zucchini |
| 4 oz (115g) mushrooms | 2 cupsful mushrooms |
| 2 peppers (1 red, 1 green) | 2 peppers (1 red, 1 green) |
| ½ lb (225g) cooked chick peas | 1 cupful cooked garbanzo beans |
| 1 teaspoonful dried mixed herbs | 1 teaspoonful dried mixed herbs |

1. Wash the rice in a sieve under running water, drain well.

2. Chop the onion, and fry with rice in the heated oil for 5 minutes, stirring. Carefully pour in the hot stock with salt, and simmer with lid on for 20 minutes.

3. Meanwhile chop the tomatoes, courgettes (zucchini), mushrooms and peppers. Add to the pan after 20 minutes, together with the cooked chick peas (garbanzos) and herbs, and simmer another 20 minutes. Check to see if rice is cooked and allow a little longer, if necessary.

*Note:* Use any kind of cooked beans or add cashews or walnuts at the end of cooking time — roughly chopped, not grated.

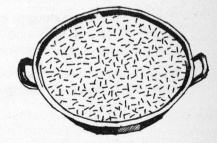

# CASHEW AND MUSHROOM CURRY *Illustrated in colour.*
## *Serves 2*

| Imperial (Metric) | American |
|---|---|
| 4 oz (115g) brown rice | ½ cupful brown rice |
| 2 medium onions | 2 medium onions |
| 1 small green pepper | 1 small green pepper |
| 3 tablespoonsful vegetable oil | 3 tablespoonsful vegetable oil |
| 2 rounded teaspoonsful curry powder (or to taste) | 2 rounded teaspoonsful curry powder (or to taste) |
| 2 rounded tablespoonsful wholemeal flour | 2 rounded tablespoonsful wholewheat flour |
| ¾ pint (425ml) hot vegetable stock or water | 2 cupsful hot vegetable stock or water |
| 2 large tomatoes | 2 large tomatoes |
| 4 oz (115g) mushrooms | 2 cupsful mushrooms |
| 1 dessert apple | 1 dessert apple |
| 1 tablespoonful raisins | 1 tablespoonful raisins |
| 4 oz (115g) broken cashew nuts | ¾ cupful broken cashew nuts |
| Squeeze of lemon juice | Squeeze of lemon juice |

1. Cook rice as described on page 24.

2. When rice is half-cooked, prepare the sauce. Chop the onions and pepper, fry gently in the heated oil and stir in the curry powder.

3. Add the flour, stir in well so that it is absorbed into the oil, then carefully pour in the hot stock, stirring till thickened. Allow to simmer gently on very low heat.

4. Chop the tomatoes, mushrooms and the unpeeled but cored apple, and add to pan with the washed raisins, nuts and lemon juice. Allow to simmer very gently with a lid on for about 15 minutes.

5. Spoon cooked rice onto a warmed dish or plates and pour the curry over it. Serve with mango chutney and green salad.

# QUICK RISOTTO
*Serves 2*

**Imperial (Metric)**
Small tin of sweet corn niblets
1 medium onion
2 courgettes or ½ cucumber
2 large tomatoes
2 tablespoonsful vegetable oil
Pinch of mixed dried herbs
2 cupsful left-over cooked rice
1 cupful left-over garden peas
4 oz (115g) roasted peanuts or
  cashews
Watercress to garnish

**American**
Small can of sweet corn niblets
1 medium onion
2 zucchini or ½ cucumber
2 large tomatoes
2 tablespoonsful vegetable oil
Pinch of mixed dried herbs
2½ cupsful left-over cooked rice
1¼ cupsful left-over garden peas
¾ cupful roasted peanuts or
  cashews
Watercress to garnish

1. Drain the tinned sweet corn.

2. Chop onion, thinly slice courgettes (zucchini) and tomatoes and gently fry in the heated oil for 3 minutes only.

3. Add herbs, rice, peas, corn and nuts, simmer gently for 2 minutes and serve garnished with watercress.

*Note:* Instead of sweet corn, stir in small tin of baked beans in tomato sauce, and omit nuts. Use a small tin of tomatoes instead of fresh, but add them last of all.

# VEGETABLE CRUMBLE
*Serves 2*

| Imperial (Metric) | American |
| --- | --- |
| 2 small leeks | 2 small leeks |
| 2 medium carrots | 2 medium carrots |
| ½ small cauliflower | ½ small cauliflower |
| 2 teaspoonsful soya sauce | 2 teaspoonsful soy sauce |
| 2 teaspoonsful polyunsaturated margarine | 2 teaspoonsful polyunsaturated margarine |
| 2 large tomatoes | 2 large tomatoes |
| Pinch of sea salt and black pepper | Pinch of sea salt and black pepper |
| 2 tablespoonsful sunflower seeds (raw or roasted) | 2 tablespoonsful sunflower seeds (raw or roasted) |
| 4 oz (115g) rolled oats | 1 cupful rolled oats |
| 2 oz (55g) polyunsaturated margarine | 5 tablespoonsful polyunsaturated margarine |
| 1 teaspoonful mixed dried herbs | 1 teaspoonful mixed dried herbs |
| 1 tablespoonful sesame seeds | 1 tablespoonful sesame seeds |

1. Thinly slice the washed leeks, carrots and cauliflower florets and stalks.

2. Put the vegetables into a saucepan with ½ pint (285ml/1⅓ cupsful) of boiling water. Put on lid, and cook on high heat for 5 minutes only. Add soya sauce and 2 teaspoonsful margarine and stir. Transfer, with liquid, to a deep ovenproof dish.

3. Slice the tomatoes and cover the dish with these, sprinkle over salt and pepper and the sunflower seeds.

4. Make a crumble topping mixing the oats, margarine, herbs and sesame seeds together with a fork in a small basin. Spoon over the dish.

5. Bake at 400°F/200°C (Gas Mark 6) for about 20 minutes until topping is crisp.

*Note:* Any mixture of vegetables of your choice, and nuts or pumpkin seeds for the topping, may be used for variety.

# MUSHROOM ROAST
*Serves 4*

| Imperial (Metric) | American |
|---|---|
| 1 large onion | 1 large onion |
| 1 small green pepper | 1 small green pepper |
| 2 oz (55g) polyunsaturated margarine | 5 tablespoonsful polyunsaturated margarine |
| ½ lb (225g) mushrooms | 4 cupsful mushrooms |
| 2 large tomatoes | 2 large tomatoes |
| ½ lb (225g) Cheddar cheese | 2 cupsful Cheddar cheese |
| 4 oz (115g) fresh wholemeal breadcrumbs | 2 cupsful fresh wholewheat breadcrumbs |
| Pinch of mixed herbs | Pinch of mixed herbs |
| Pinch of black pepper | Pinch of black pepper |
| 2 tablespoonsful chopped parsley | 2 tablespoonsful chopped parsley |
| 1 tablespoonful raw sesame seeds | 1 tablespoonful raw sesame seeds |

1.  Chop onion and pepper and fry in heated margarine for 2 minutes only in a large saucepan. Slice mushrooms and add to pan, stir for 1 minute only. Remove from heat.

2.  Chop the tomatoes, grate the cheese (reserve 2 tablespoonsful for topping), add to saucepan with crumbs, herbs, pepper and parsley.

3.  Mix well, but carefully, and spoon into an oiled, deep ovenproof dish, sprinkle on the remainder of the cheese and the sesame seeds. Bake at 375°F/190°C (Gas Mark 5) for about 20 minutes.

# 7.

# VEGETABLES AND SALADS

## WAYS WITH VEGETABLES

There must be hundreds of ways to serve vegetables as side dishes — here are just a few.

- Serve lightly fried mushrooms stirred into cooked Brussels sprouts, or garnish a dish of sprouts with toasted flaked almonds.
- Garden peas with chopped chives, or finely chopped onion and a little grated orange peel.
- Steamed cabbage tossed in a little margarine and sprinkled with caraway seeds; or mixed with fried onions, tomatoes and a little basil.
- Steamed fennel bulbs with margarine or cheese sauce, or allowed to cool and served with Oil and Lemon Dressing (page 83) as a salad or a starter.
- Parsnips or carrots, scrubbed, trimmed and spread with margarine, wrapped in foil, and baked in oven till tender — about 45-60 minutes in a medium hot oven.
- Corn on the cob. Keep husk and silky threads on the cob until ready to use. Remove these and plunge the cob into boiling water (do not add salt, it toughens the kernels) just add a squeeze of lemon juice, and cook 8 minutes only, remove, drain briefly, insert cob forks and serve with margarine or butter.
- Cook chopped red cabbage in water or apple juice, with a pinch each of nutmeg and thyme. Cook 2 chopped apples in orange juice (reserve strips of orange peel for garnish). *Purée* the apples

and spoon on top of the cooked cabbage in a serving dish. Garnish with orange strips and parsley sprigs.

- Cooked, diced beetroots (beets) in an ovenproof dish, coated with a sauce of yogurt with chopped chives, and a pinch each of cinnamon, nutmeg and black pepper mixed in, covered with a lid or foil and baked in medium oven for 20 minutes, is delicious.

- Aubergines (eggplants) sometimes have a bitter taste after cooking, but if you halve them lengthways, sprinkle with salt, leave for 30 minutes or so, wash away the salt, and dry surface with paper towel, you can proceed with any recipe, without the bitterness.

- Potatoes, Jacket-baked: Simply scrub well with a vegetable brush, trim if necessary, make holes in the potatoes with a fork or knife, to stop them bursting, and put on a tray in the oven. For a softer skin, as above, then brush with oil and bake; or brush with oil and cover with foil and bake.

- Bircher Potatoes: Scrub and trim as above, halve lengthways. Mix 1 teaspoonful caraway seeds and ½ teaspoonful salt on a plate, dip cut side of potato into mixture and place on a well-oiled baking tray. Brush tops with oil and bake for an hour or so at 375°F/190°C (Gas Mark 5) till tender.

# AVOCADO AND ORANGE SALAD

**Imperial (Metric)**
1 lettuce heart or 1 head chicory
1 ripe avocado pear
1 large orange
Cress to garnish
Oil and Lemon Dressing (page 83)

**American**
1 lettuce heart or 1 head chicory
1 ripe avocado pear
1 large orange
Cress to garnish
Oil and Lemon Dressing (page 83)

1.  Arrange the lettuce or chicory leaves on a dish.

2.  Skin and stone the avocado, and cut into slices.

3.  Remove all skin, pith and pips from the orange, and separate into segments.

4.  Place alternate slices of avocado and orange in a pattern around the dish. Heap cress into the centre and sprinkle with dressing.

# CELERY COLESLAW

**Imperial (Metric)**
1 large head celery
1 large chunk white cabbage
2 firm tomatoes
1 large onion
½ green pepper
Oil and vinegar dressing
Black pepper
French mustard

**American**
1 large head celery
1 large chunk white cabbage
2 firm tomatoes
1 large onion
½ green pepper
Oil and vinegar dressing
Black pepper
French mustard

1.  Wash, trim and chop the celery. Shred the cabbage. Chop the tomatoes, onion and pepper.

2.  Mix the dressing with the pepper and mustard, and gently stir in all the vegetables.

# BEETROOT AND APPLE SALAD

| Imperial (Metric) | American |
|---|---|
| Raw or cooked beetroots | Raw or cooked beets |
| Dessert or cooking apples | Dessert or cooking apples |
| Oil and Lemon Dressing (page 83) | Oil and Lemon Dressing (page 83) |
| Chives, parsley or onion rings | Chives, parsley or onion rings |

1. Coarsely grate equal quantities of beetroot (beet) and apple into a salad bowl.

2. Mix in salad dressing and garnish with chopped chives or parsley, or onion rings.


# BEAN, TOMATO AND RICE SALAD *Illustrated in colour.*

| Imperial (Metric) | American |
|---|---|
| 4 tablespoonsful cooked rice | 4 tablespoonsful cooked rice |
| 2 tomatoes | 2 tomatoes |
| 1 green or red pepper | 1 green or red pepper |
| ½ small cucumber | ½ small cucumber |
| 14 oz (400g) tin beans (red kidney, cannellini etc.) | 1 medium can beans (red kidney, cannellini etc.) |
| Dressing of choice | Dressing of choice |
| Fresh herbs (optional) | Fresh herbs (optional) |

1. Put the rice into a bowl.

2. Chop the tomatoes, cut the pepper into thin strips, cut the cucumber into small dice. Add to bowl and mix.

3. Drain and rinse the tin of beans and add to bowl.

4. Pour on a little dressing and mix gently. Snip fresh herbs to garnish.

# CAULIFLOWER, CARROT AND CUCUMBER SALAD

| Imperial (Metric) | American |
|---|---|
| ½ small cauliflower | ½ small cauliflower |
| 2 medium carrots | 2 medium carrots |
| Small piece of cucumber | Small piece of cucumber |
| Dressing | Dressing |
| Watercress to garnish | Watercress to garnish |

1. Wash and drain the cauliflower. Break into florets and slice these and stalks into a bowl.

2. Coarsely grate the carrots, or cut into matchsticks. Add to bowl.

3. Cut cucumber into matchsticks and add to bowl.

4. Add dressing of choice and mix well. Garnish with watercress.


# WINTER SALAD  *Illustrated in colour.*

| Imperial (Metric) | American |
|---|---|
| 10 washed Brussels sprouts | 10 washed Brussels sprouts |
| 1 medium onion | 1 medium onion |
| 1 small washed turnip | 1 small washed turnip |
| 3 medium carrots | 3 medium carrots |
| Dressing of choice | Dressing of choice |
| Herbs | Herbs |

1. Finely shred the sprouts and the onion. Grate the turnip and the carrots.

2. Mix in a bowl with the dressing and herbs of your choice.

*Note:* Inner cabbage leaves may be used instead of Brussels sprouts.

# CELERIAC SALAD

| Imperial (Metric) | American |
|---|---|
| 1 small celeriac root | 1 small celeriac root |
| 2 medium carrots | 2 medium carrots |
| 1 medium onion | 1 medium onion |
| Dressing of choice | Dressing of choice |
| Parsley and cress to garnish | Parsley and cress to garnish |

1. Wash, trim and finely grate the celeriac. Grate the carrots coarsely and finely chop the onion.

2. Mix together with the dressing and garnish with parsley and cress.

# FENNEL AND CUCUMBER SALAD

| Imperial (Metric) | American |
|---|---|
| 1 small fennel bulb | 1 small fennel bulb |
| Piece of cucumber | Piece of cucumber |
| 1 cupful cooked peas | 1 cupful cooked peas |
| Dressing of choice | Dressing of choice |
| Tomato chunks to garnish | Tomato chunks to garnish |

1. Wash, trim and finely slice the fennel. Dice the cucumber.

2. Mix together in a bowl with the peas and dressing. Garnish.

*Note:* If the peas are freshly picked from your own garden, they will have a lovely flavour and texture left raw.

## CHINESE SALAD *Illustrated in colour.*

| Imperial (Metric) | American |
|---|---|
| 1 cupful beansprouts | 1¼ cupsful beansprouts |
| ½ small Chinese cabbage (Chinese leaves) | ½ small Chinese cabbage (Chinese leaves) |
| 4 mushrooms | 4 mushrooms |
| 8 spring onions | 8 scallions |
| 3 sticks celery | 3 stalks celery |
| Oil and Lemon Dressing (page 83) | Oil and Lemon Dressing (page 83) |
| 1 banana | 1 banana |
| 1 tablespoonful roasted cashew nuts | 1 tablespoonful roasted cashew nuts |
| 1 tablespoonful flaked almonds | 1 tablespoonful slivered almonds |
| Celery leaves to garnish | Celery leaves to garnish |

1. Wash and drain the beansprouts and Chinese cabbage. Shred the cabbage leaves roughly and add these two ingredients to bowl.

2. Slice the onions and celery into long thin strips. Slice the mushrooms thinly and add these ingredients to the bowl with a little dressing. Mix well with a fork.

3. Add the sliced banana and the nuts and mix.

4. Add more dressing if needed. Spoon onto a serving dish and garnish with celery leaves.

# OIL AND LEMON DRESSING

**Imperial (Metric)**
1 tablespoonful freshly squeezed
   lemon juice
3 tablespoonsful vegetable oil
   (sunflower, corn or olive)
Pinch of sea salt and black pepper
Tiny pinch of Demerara sugar if
   desired

**American**
1 tablespoonful freshly squeezed
   lemon juice
3 tablespoonsful vegetable oil
   (sunflower, corn or olive)
Pinch of sea salt and black pepper
Tiny pinch of Demerara sugar if
   desired

Pour all ingredients into a small jar with the screw-top lid firmly placed, and shake well. Use within 2-3 days, but keep in the refrigerator or a very cold place meanwhile.

*Note:* Multiply amount, as required, and add made mustard, fresh or dried herbs, if liked. Cider vinegar, red or white wine vinegar could be used instead of lemon juice.

# YOGURT DRESSING

**Imperial (Metric)**
1 small carton natural yogurt
1 teaspoonful finely chopped mint or
   herb of choice
Pinch of sea salt and black pepper
2 teaspoonsful freshly squeezed
   lemon juice

**American**
1 small carton natural yogurt
1 teaspoonful finely chopped mint or
   herb of choice
Pinch of sea salt and black pepper
2 teaspoonsful freshly squeezed
   lemon juice

Mix all ingredients together in a small bowl with a wooden spoon. Use the same day as made, but keep covered in the refrigerator until needed.

*Note:* 1 teaspoonful curry paste blended into the yogurt, without the herbs, can be used.

# HOT AND COLD YOGURT DRESSING

**Imperial (Metric)**
1 small carton of natural yogurt
2 tablespoonsful grated horseradish
Pinch of sea salt and black pepper
Pinch of cayenne pepper (beware —
    very hot!)
2 teaspoonsful freshly squeezed
    lemon juice

**American**
1 small carton of natural yogurt
2 tablespoonsful grated horseradish
Pinch of sea salt and black pepper
Pinch of cayenne pepper (beware —
    very hot!)
2 teaspoonsful freshly squeezed
    lemon juice

1.  Mix all ingredients together in a small bowl with a wooden spoon.
    Use the same day as made, but keep covered in the refrigerator
    until needed.

# 8.

# DESSERTS

Most home-made dessert ingredients can be adapted to appeal to a vegetarian — use only vegetable fats and oils, wholemeal or 81% flours, free-range eggs, raw cane sugar (which can be made finer in a blender), agar agar instead of gelatine etc. But here are some easy and delicious fruit-based desserts for you to try.

## FRESH FRUIT SALAD

Wash, peel if necessary, and slice or dice any fresh fruit, arrange in glass bowl, pour in apple juice, or orange juice, or mix orange and pineapple juices. Please do not add sugar or sugar syrup, it spoils the fresh flavours.

The combinations of fruit are almost endless, and if you cannot buy all the fresh fruit you'd like, use some canned fruit in its own juice — such as pineapple and peaches instead. Garnish the bowl with washed strawberry leaves or fresh mint leaves.

## FRUIT JELLY  *Illustrated in colour.*
*Serves 4*

| Imperial (Metric) | American |
| --- | --- |
| 2 rounded teaspoonsful powdered agar-agar | 2 rounded teaspoonsful powdered agar-agar |
| Approx. 3 tablespoonsful cold water | Approx. 3 tablespoonsful cold water |
| ½ pint (285ml) boiling water | 1⅓ cupsful boiling water |
| 2 rounded dessertspoonsful Demerara sugar or maple syrup | 4 rounded teaspoonsful Demerara sugar or maple syrup |
| ½ pint (285ml) fresh orange or pineapple juice | 1⅓ cupsful fresh orange or pineapple juice |
| Fresh fruit of choice | Fresh fruit of choice |

1. Put the agar-agar into a bowl with the cold water. Mix and leave to stand for 10 minutes. Add more water if the mixture becomes too solid.

2. Pour on the boiling water and sugar or syrup, stir well, and pour into a saucepan. Boil for one minute, stirring well.

3. Remove from heat, cool for 2-3 minutes. Add the fruit juice and stir well. Add any chopped pieces of fresh fruit desired, before pouring into a fancy mould or individual dishes. Serve with Cashew Nut Cream (page 89).

## APPLE AND DATE WHIP
*Serves 4*

| Imperial (Metric) | American |
| --- | --- |
| 2 large cooking apples | 2 large cooking apples |
| ½ lb (225g) stoned dates | 1½ cupsful stoned dates |
| 1 tablespoonful coconut cream | 1 tablespoonful coconut cream |
| Juice of an orange and a little grated rind | Juice of an orange and a little grated rind |

1. Wash and chop apples and dates, and cook in a little water until very soft.

2.  Beat in coconut cream and orange juice whilst mixture is still hot.

3.  Spoon into individual dishes and garnish with the orange rind.

# BAKED BANANAS WITH PLUM SAUCE
*Serves 4*

| **Imperial (Metric)** | **American** |
|---|---|
| 4 large bananas | 4 large bananas |
| ½ pint (285ml) orange juice | 1⅓ cupsful orange juice |
| Pinch of ground cloves or cinnamon | Pinch of ground cloves or cinnamon |
| 1 lb (455g) red plums | 1 pound red plums |
| 1 dessertspoonful dark raw cane sugar (or pure maple syrup) | 2 teaspoonsful dark raw cane sugar (or pure maple syrup) |

1.  Peel the bananas, slice lengthways and arrange in an ovenproof dish. Sprinkle on ground cloves or cinnamon, and pour on orange juice. Bake at 350°F/180°C (Gas Mark 4) for about 20 minutes.

2.  Meanwhile wash, halve and stone the plums. Cook in a saucepan with a little water and the sugar.

3.  When tender, liquidize, or mash with a potato masher, or push through a sieve over a basin, with a spoon, to make them smooth. Heat gently and pour into a jug to serve.

*Note:* In the winter, a tin of plums could be used.

# APRICOT AND APPLE DELIGHT
*Serves 4*

| Imperial (Metric) | American |
|---|---|
| ½ lb (225g) dried apricots | 1½ cupsful dried apricots |
| ½ pint (285ml) orange juice | 1⅓ cupsful orange juice |
| 2 large cooking apples | 2 large cooking apples |
| 1 tablespoonful pure maple syrup | 1 tablespoonful pure maple syrup |
| A few pistachio nuts | A few pistachio nuts |

1. Wash, chop, and soak the apricots in the orange juice overnight. Liquidize, or push through a sieve over a basin with a spoon, and set aside.

2. Chop and cook the apples with the maple syrup until very soft. Liquidize as above.

3. Put alternate layers of apricot and apple *purées* into tall glasses and garnish with finely sliced pistachio nuts.


# PEARS IN CINNAMON SAUCE
*Serves 4*

| Imperial (Metric) | American |
|---|---|
| 4 large pears | 4 large pears |
| ½ pint (285ml) water | 1⅓ cupsful water |
| 2 tablespoonsful pure maple syrup | 2 tablespoonsful pure maple syrup |
| 1 level teaspoonful powdered cinnamon | 1 level teaspoonful powdered cinnamon |
| 1 tablespoonful raisins | 1 tablespoonful raisins |
| 1 tablespoonful flaked almonds | 1 tablespoonful slivered almonds |

1. Put the water, maple syrup and cinnamon in a large saucepan, stir and heat gently.

2. Peel, halve and core the pears, add to pan, and spoon the liquid over them. Put on the lid, and simmer till tender (about 30-40 minutes). Spoon liquid over the pears occasionally.

3. Put the raisins in a cup, pour on boiling water to just cover them. Set aside.

4. When the pears are tender (test with a sharp knife), spoon into individual serving dishes, with any liquid left, and garnish with the soaked raisins and the almonds.

## CASHEW NUT CREAM

| Imperial (Metric) | American |
|---|---|
| 4 oz (115g) broken cashew nuts | ¾ cupful broken cashew nuts |
| 6 tablespoonsful cold water | 6 tablespoonsful cold water |
| 3 teaspoonsful vegetable oil | 3 teaspoonsful vegetable oil |
| 1 large banana | 1 large banana |
| A few drops of pure vanilla essence | A few drops of pure vanilla essence |

1. Grate the cashew nuts to a fine powder in a blender or food processor.

2. Add the water, oil, chopped skinned banana, and vanilla.

3. Blend until thick and smooth. Add more water if the cream is too thick for your purpose.

# FRUIT AND NUT BARS

| Imperial (Metric) | American |
|---|---|
| 6 oz (170g) stoned dates | 1 cupful stoned dates |
| 6 oz (170g) dried apricots | 1 cupful dried apricots |
| 2 oz (55g) cashew nuts | ⅓ cupful cashew nuts |
| 2 oz (55g) hazelnuts | ⅓ cupful hazelnuts |
| 2 teaspoonsful grated orange rind and all the juice of a small orange | 2 teaspoonsful grated orange rind and all the juice of a small orange |

1. Wash dates and apricots, drain well and allow to dry out. Chop finely and put through a mincer into a large mixing bowl.

2. Grind the nuts finely in a mouli-mill. Add to bowl.

3. Wash the orange, grate a little rind (a zester is a useful tool here), then cut the orange in half and squeeze the juice into bowl and add rind.

4. Blend all ingredients with a potato masher or fork.

5. Line a shallow baking tin with a sheet of rice paper, spoon mixture in carefully, and flatten it evenly. Add a top sheet of rice paper. Allow to firm up. Cut into size required with hot, sharp knife.

*Note:* Any dried fruit or nuts can be used for these delicious little bars: prunes; raisins; currants; sultanas (golden seedless raisins); figs; dried apples; pears; bananas etc. And for variety, you could also coarsely grate some of the nuts you add, or use sunflower or pumpkin seeds, raw or toasted, to make the bars more crunchy. The mixture can also be rolled into large marbles and coated with chopped nuts, to serve as petit fours.

# GLOSSARY OF WORDS OFTEN HEARD ON THE VEGETARIAN SCENE

**Barley Flakes** are partly cooked barley grains.

**Buckwheat** (Saracen Corn) when roasted is known as **kasha.**

**Bulgur** (burghul) is partly cooked **cracked wheat.**

**Carob bean** (locust bean or St John's Bread) is powdered for use in cakes, biscuits, desserts, bars and drinks etc., and is close in taste to cocoa or chocolate.

**Chinese five-spice powder** is equal parts of finely ground anise, star anise, cassia or cinnamon, cloves and fennel seed.

**Coriander leaves** (cilantro) or Chinese Parsley — the leaves have an orange taste and are used in curries and for garnishing.

**Coriander seeds** are powdered for sweet and savoury dishes.

**Garam masala** means 'hot mixture' and is a curry mix of coriander seed, chili and black pepper, usually.

**Groats** are whole oat grains.

**Laver** is Welsh seaweed.

**Malt extract** is the soluble part of the malted (soaked) grain, and is extracted and evaporated.

**Miso** is a thick brown paste used for soups, sauces, spreads etc. **Mugi Miso** is made from soya beans and barley and fermented for one year, **Kome Miso** is made from soya beans and rice and fermented for one year, **Hatcho Miso** is made with soya beans only and fermented for three years. All are very salty — when using add no other salt.

**Mu tea** is made from 16 herbs, and has a gingery-licorice taste.

**Nori** is seaweed in thin brittle sheets. It turns from black to brilliant green when toasted over a naked flame, at which point it is ready for use, broken over a rice and vegetable dish.

**Soya Sauce, Shoyu** and **Tamari** are made from soya beans, wheat, sea salt and water and fermented for two years.

**Soya flour** is made from ground soya beans and is heat treated.

**Soya grits** are soya beans broken into tiny pieces which are quick-cooking.

**Soya milk** is made from soya beans and water. It comes in cans (to be diluted) and cartons ready to use.

**Soya milk powder** is especially useful for feeding babies and others allergic to other milks.

**Soya protein** or **textured vegetable protein (tvp)** is made from soya beans, often to resemble meat products, such as mince, chunks, burgermix, and sausages.

**Tahini** is sesame paste, made by crushing sesame seeds.

**Tofu** is a white soft soya bean curd used to make sweet and savoury dishes. It needs a strong flavour added to it.

**Umembosi** (Umeboshi) are Japanese pickled plums used as a seasoning in grain or vegetable dishes.

**Wheat berries** are whole wheat grains.

**Wheatgerm** is the 'heart' of the wheat grain not found in white flour.

# USEFUL ADDRESSES

Organizations concerned with animals, farming, food and health:

Henry Doubleday Research Association (advises on organic growing), Ryton on Dunsmore, Coventry, CV8 3LG.

Beauty Without Cruelty Ltd. (company producing cruelty-free cosmetics), Avebury Avenue, Tonbridge, Kent.

British College of Naturopathy and Osteopathy, 6 Netherhall Gardens, London, NW3 5RR.

British Homoeopathic Association, 27a Devonshire Street, London, W1.

Chickens' Lib, 6 Pilling Lane, Skelmansthorpe, Huddersfield, West Yorks.

Compassion in World Farming, 20 Lavant Street, Petersfield, Hants.

Farm and Food Society, 4 Willifield Way, London, NW11 7XT.

FREGG (Free Range Egg Association), 39 Maresfield Gardens, London NW3.

Friends of the Earth, 377, City Road, London EC1V 1NA.

National Society Against Factory Farming, 42 Mount Pleasant Road, London SE13.

Organic Growers' Association, Aeron Park, Llangeitho, Dyfed.

The Soil Association (advises on organic farming and growing), 86-88 Colston Street, Bristol, BS1 5BB.

The Vegetarian Society U.K. Limited, Parkdale, Dunham Road, Altrincham, Cheshire, WA14 4QG.

The Vegan Society (advises on vegan diet), 7 Battle Road, St. Leonards-on-Sea, East Sussex, TN37 7AA.

Vegetarian Times Magazine, P.O. Box 570, Oak Park, Illinois 60302.

PLEASE SEND A STAMPED ADDRESSED ENVELOPE WITH EVERY ENQUIRY.

# WHERE CAN I TURN FOR HELP?

The Vegetarian Society of course!

In return for a large stamped self-addressed envelope with two loose first class stamps, they will send you free literature which includes a book list and recipes. The Society also operates a free information service on vegetarian matters, but please enclose a stamped addressed envelope with all enquiries.

The Vegetarian Society welcomes new members and associates, who receive a copy of *The Vegetarian* magazine by post every two months.

*The Vegetarian* brings you news, views, recipes, special series and articles on animal welfare, ecology, health, slimming, self-sufficiency and organic gardening, as well as special offers and competitions.

Information on vegetarian restaurants, hotels, guest houses, health food and wholefood stores, health centres and hydros, and food additives, can be found in the Society's *International Vegetarian Handbook*, published bi-annually, with interim supplement. It also contains a Shopper's Guide section listing a wide range of products acceptable to vegetarians and vegans along with other details which are invaluable for everyone concerned with healthy eating. Write to either:

The Vegetarian Society U.K. Ltd.,
Parkdale,
Dunham Road,
Altrincham,
Cheshire WA14 4QG.

# INDEX

Aduki Burgers, 58
Almond and Potato Loaf, 62
Almonds, Blanched, 27
*Animal Liberation*, 9
Apple and Date Whip, 86
Apricot and Apple Delight, 88
Avocado and Orange Salad, 78

Bananas with Plum Sauce, Baked, 87
Bean, Tomato and Rice Salad, 79
beans, 23-4
Beetroot and Apple Salad, 79
Breadcrumbs, 33

Cashew and Mushroom Curry, 72
Cashew Nut Cream, 89
Cauliflower, Carrot and Cucumber
  Salad, 80
Celeriac Salad, 81
Celery Coleslaw, 78
Cheese and Apple Toast, 46
Cheese, Apple and Beetroot Flan, 70
Cheese Sauce, Rich Quick, 31
Chick Pea Croquettes, 61
Chick Pea with Rice, 71
Chinese Salad, 82
Chinese Stir-Fry, 51
Croutons, 33
Crumbles, 33

Date and Nut Spread, 43

diet plans, 11-14

Fennel and Cucumber Salad, 81
food storage, 20
Fruit and Nut Bars, 90
Fruit Jelly, 86
Fruit, Nut and Milk Shake, 52
Fruit Salad, Fresh, 85
Fruity Black-Eye Beans, 57

Golden Slice, 56
Goma Sio, 44
Guacamole Dip or Spread, 42

Hazelnut Spread, 42
Hummus, 41
Hungarian Bean Loaf, 65

*International Vegetarian Handbook*,
  16, 20, 94

Julienne Soup, 37

kitchen tools, 21

Leek and Carrot Soup, 34
Lentil and Tomato Bake, 64
Lentil Paste, 40
Lentil Paste with Mushrooms on
  Toast, 46
Lunches, Packed, 53
  Quick, 44-5

Macaroni Cheese Special, 60
Muesli, 29, 52
Mushroom Pizza, 66
Mushroom Roast, 75

Nuts and Seeds, Roasted, 27
Nutty Fries, 49

Oil and Lemon Dressing, 83

Pan Haggerty, 50
Pastes, Home-made, 39
Pastry, Wholemeal, 28
Pea Soup, Minty Green, 36
Pears in Cinnamon Sauce, 88
Potatoes, Jacket-baked, 77
　Bircher, 77

Ratatouille, 63
Rice, Brown, 24
　Fried and Boiled Brown, 25
　Plain Boiled Brown, 24
Rice Croquettes, 59
Risotto, Quick, 73

Salad, Winter, 80

Sauce, Rich Brown, 32
Sauce, Tangy, 32
Seeds for Sprouting, 26
Sesame and Brazil Nut Roast, 54-5
Spaghetti Neapolitan, 47
Starters, Fresh and Tangy, 38

Tomato and Mushroom Savoury, 45
Tomato Sauce, 31
Tomato Soup, Fresh, 35
Tomatoes, 27

Vegetable Crumble, 74
Vegetables, 76-7
Vegetables, Stuffed, 67-9
Vegetarian Society, The, 18-19, 94
　cookery courses, 18-19
　membership, 19
*Vegetarian, The*, 94

Welsh Rarebit Special, 48
White Sauce, Basic, 30
　Whisked, 30

Yogurt Dressing, 83
　Hot and Cold, 84